HORTEN Ho 229

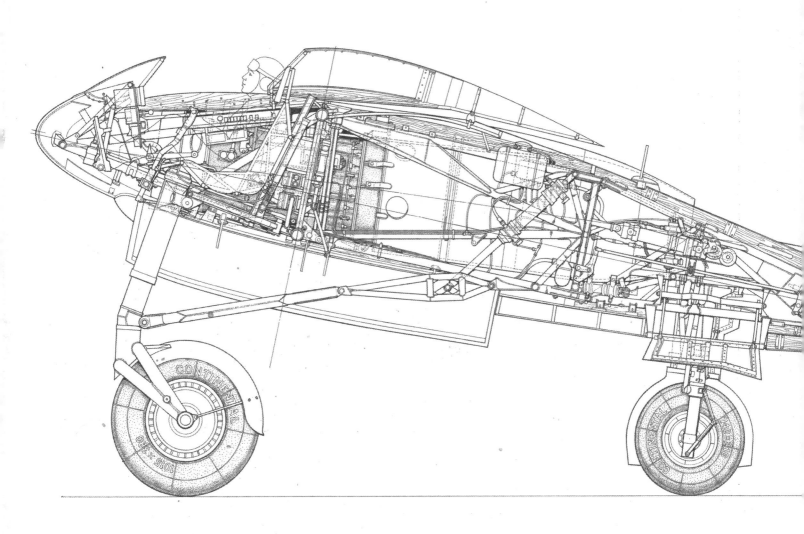

Dedicated to the all the 'Flying Brothers' who wrote their stories

for the History of Aviation:

The Montgolfier brothers

The Wright brothers

The Voisin brothers

The Nieuport brothers

The Farman brothers

The Short brothers

The Granville brothers

The Horten brothers (and sister)

The Günter brothers (Heinkel Flugzeugbau)

The Hütter brothers (Schempp-Hirth Segelflugzeugbau)

The Loughead (Lockheed) brothers

The Dittmar brothers

The Rutan brothers

The Schweizer brothers

The Loening brothers

The Miles brothers

and many others…

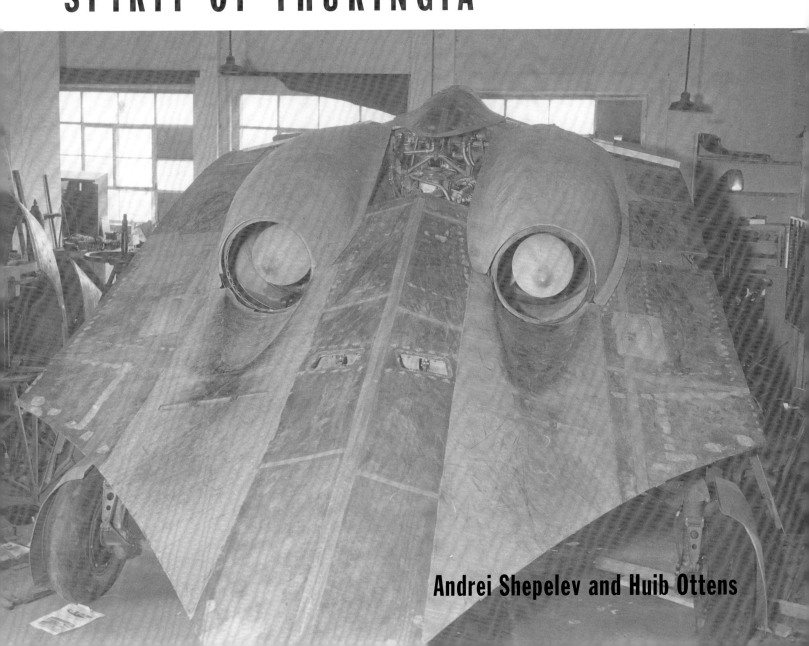

CLASSIC
An imprint of
Crécy Publishing Ltd

HORTEN Ho 229

SPIRIT OF THURINGIA

The Horten All-Wing Jet Fighter

Andrei Shepelev and Huib Ottens

Andrei Shepelev has been interested in aviation, especially in unconventional and lesser-known designs, since an early age, and as an aircraft modeller. He is a former student of the Kuibyshev Aviation Institution, specialising in spacecraft and rocket technology and has worked for a number of publishing organisations as an editor and designer. He is married and has a son and two daughters and lives in Russia.

Huib Ottens first became interested in aviation when he read Biggles stories as a boy. He has a particular interest in the history of the *Luftwaffe* and has been researching the history of the Horten Brothers and their flying wing designs for some 20 years. He lives with his partner and their two children in Holland and works as a systems designer and developer for the IT department of a large Dutch bank.

Acknowledgements

The authors wish to acknowledge the following individuals for their kind help in the preparation of this work:

In Germany: Manfred Boehme, Hartmut Küper, Prof. Dr. Karl Nickel, Gunilde Nickel-Horten, Winfried Römer, Peter F. Selinger, Reinhold Stadler, Ewald Uden, Gerd Zipper

In the USA: Albion H. Bowers, Mark Cowan, Richard T. Eger, Kenneth Kik, Richard Kik Jr., Russell E. Lee, David Myhra, Geoff Steele

In Belgium: Eric du Trieu de Terdonck

In Great Britain: Arthur Bentley, Robert Forsyth, Eddie J. Creek, Paul Williams

In Australia: Alan Scheckenbach

In Spain: Raul Escapa

Horten Ho 229
© 2006 Andrei Shepelev and Huib Ottens

First published 2006
First reprint 2014
Second reprint 2015

ISBN 978 1 903223 66 6

Produced by Chevron Publishing Limited
Project Editors: Chevron Publishing Limited
Book design: Mark Nelson

© Colour artwork: Andrei Shepelev
© Technical drawings: Arthur Bentley
The line drawings produced in this book by Arthur Bentley
as well as his other extensive aviation line art can be ordered
from www.albentley-drawings.com

© Crécy Publishing Ltd 2015
Published by Crécy Publishing
1a Ringway Trading Estate
Shadowmoss Rd
Manchester
M22 5LH
www.crecy.co.uk

Printed in Malta by Melita Press

CLASSIC
An imprint of
Crécy Publishing Ltd

Horten Flugzeugbau G.m.b.H. Bonn, Venusbergweg 12

Postscheckkonto: Köln 30781
Deutsche Bank, Filiale Bonn 108034
Fernruf: 8498
Venusbergweg 12

⊕ BONN

Ihr Schreiben: Ihr Zeichen: Unser Schreiben: Unser Zeichen:

CONTENTS

**Foreword
by
Karl Nickel**

When looking at the designs of aircraft since the end of the Second World War one finds many extremely interesting new designs and developments. If one restricts oneself to the area of military fighters one finds that this region is especially interesting. But of all the fighter-bombers which have been designed and built during the last 65 years there is, however, one model which is quite outstanding in every respect. This is the Horten H IX, also known as the Ho 229. No other aircraft exists which can be compared with it. Even an unbiased observer sees immediately by looking at pictures of this bird the qualities of elegance, simplicity, avoidance of all superfluous parts and of any unnecessary drag, clear lines and a certain streamlined beauty.

I am quite happy to see that Andrei Shepelev and Huib Ottens pay tribute to this aerodynamic marvel and bring it to the public eye.

I enjoy this fact even more because part of my own life is interwoven with this wonder of technology and with the two Horten brothers. It has namely been my own duty between the years of 1943 and 1945 to make extensive calculations for the H IX with respect to dimensioning of the spars and the shell by computing the stress and strain, ensuring stability and finally to evaluate and to predict performance.

This book contains much information for both the expert and the interested layman. Therefore I wish it the success which it deserves!

Karl Nickel

*Freiburg i.Br.
Germany*

Prof. Dr. Karl Nickel has unfortunately passed away on 1 January 2009

THE history of aviation is full of great ideas. Some of the ideas from the early pioneers have survived to this day; others have been passed by as too difficult to create with current technology, and some have just proven to be outright wrong. But in the Pantheon of truly great revolutionary ideas, there are few.

Over one hundred years ago, two brothers decided to create practical flight. Their innovations and approach survive to this day. These two brothers, Orville and Wilbur Wright, and their ideas, are generally recognized by history and by nearly all scientists and engineers as being the first truly practical approach to flight. The Wrights created flight by breaking the necessary components of flight down to their respective parts. They solved the problems of structure, propulsion, stability, control, and performance. To do this, they started with the fundamentals they observed from the flight of birds. One of the great leaps forward the Wrights made was when they shook off the illusion of mechanical flight as being simply an extension of two-dimensional travel, namely railroad technology. They saw the problem of flight as being one of banking the aircraft to turn it. In so doing, it was necessary to invent the vertical tail and three-axis control. This is the same thing most aeronautical engineers do today to design aircraft. But with the Wrights doing this, the flight of birds was left behind as the ideal model for flight. This was how the Wrights flew, for the first time, at Kitty Hawk, North Carolina in 1903.

One of the discoveries the Wrights made was that with roll control there is a dramatic tendency for the roll to cause a yaw motion in the direction opposite to the turn. This is called adverse yaw, and it is the primary function of the rudder to overcome the adverse yaw. Every student pilot has adverse yaw drilled into their heads and soon kicking the rudder, with aileron roll input, becomes automatic. This is more prevalent in aircraft with large or long wings and small or short tails (sailplanes exhibit this tendency more than most other kinds of aircraft for exactly this reason). What is happening is that the wing creates more lift to move up and creates more drag, and so is moved aft. This idea of roll control is exactly what the Wrights patented, the idea of bank-to-turn, not the idea of the propeller aircraft.

Now ask yourself, when was the last time you saw a bird with a vertical tail? What is it that birds know that we do not?

Enter one of the great minds, if not the greatest mind, of all aeronautics – this is the true father of modern design theory for aircraft: Dr. Ludwig Prandtl. Prandtl invented the lifting line theory to explain and model how wings create lift. With a working theory of how wings worked, Prandtl then theorized and obtained the optimum wing load distribution across the span to minimize the drag created by the lift of the wing. This drag is seen as wingtip vortices and is called induced drag. The energy left in these vortices is energy taken from the wing as it passes through the air.

The optimum solution was published by Prandtl in 1918. The optimum shape of the spanload is elliptical. This solution is so compelling that even today most textbooks refer to the elliptical spanwise load for the wing as the optimum, without stating what it is the optimum for. This optimum is the minimum drag for a wing of a given span and a given lift. But Prandtl did not stop there. In 1933, he published a little known paper in German, the title of which is translated as '*The Minimum Induced Drag of Wings.*' Why would Prandtl rescind his earlier optimum elliptical spanload for a different new one?

This new spanload considered a different case. Prandtl asked himself, given an elliptical spanload as optimum for a given span, is there a different spanload which would give the same bending moment at the root of the wing as the elliptical spanload and have the same lift, that would create less induced drag? The wing root bending moment is the primary consideration given to the size of the structure required to hold the wing together, the wing spar. With Prandtl's lifting line theory, this could be investigated. The new optimum spanload, considering the wing root bending moment, was not elliptical but was bell-shaped. The results of Prandtl's analysis showed that for the same lift and the same wing root bending moment, a 22 per cent increase in span resulted in an 11 per cent decrease in induced drag. Prandtl's paper was not given much recognition (not even today), but the implications are vast and far reaching, and even Prandtl did not realize it.

In 1932, there were two other brothers who began to investigate the possibilities of flight. These brothers were Reimar and Walter Horten. Their first aircraft, a small sailplane, was an all flying wing, with no vertical surfaces at all. This first Horten sailplane did not use Prandtl's new bell-shaped spanload (it would not be called bell-shaped until years later, and then it was only called this by Reimar Horten), and it did not fly well. But the Hortens, particularly Reimar, were persistent and solved the problems of flying wings one at a time. The optimum bell-shaped spanload later solved the problems of directional stability, and helped to minimize the structure needed for their long wing sailplanes. The problem of adverse yaw would plague their aircraft all through their years together in Germany, through World War Two, followed Reimar through his PhD, and even to his move to Argentina after the war. Reimar continued to design and build sailplanes. The final solution came to Reimar while he was in Argentina, the solution to the adverse yaw problem. There were a handful of designs from Horten in Argentina that solved all the great problems of the all flying wing aircraft (even sailplanes) and required no vertical tail.

The solution lay in how the wingtip vortices are treated. With the bell-shaped spanload, the vortices act on the wingtips more strongly than in the elliptical spanload case. The result is that the lift at the wingtips is influenced by the wingtip vortices,

An Introduction
by
Albion H Bowers

"When was the last time you saw a bird with a vertical tail?"

Dr. Ludwig Prandtl.

and the lift is rotated far more forward than in the case of the elliptical spanload. Now, instead of creating more drag with more lift, because the lift is rotated forward from the effect of the wingtip vortices, the greater lift overcomes the greater drag and the wing that moves up creates induced thrust *forward*. Roll is coupled to yaw in a proverse way, not adverse; and the vertical tail is rendered superfluous. But this proverse yaw can only happen if the part of the wing creating the greater lift is at the very tips of the wings: all the roll control must reside near the very ends of the wingtips while using the bell-shaped spanload. Dr. Reimar Horten had used Dr. Ludwig Prandtl's bell-shaped spanload to optimize the drag, minimize the structure, solve the problem for minimum control surfaces and eliminate the vertical tail.

Again, when was the last time you saw a bird with a vertical tail?

For birds to survive, they too must be optimal in all these same ways. For a bird to carry unnecessary body parts means the design of such a bird is not optimal to fit into its ecological niche. Such an animal would become extinct quickly. The chest muscles of the bird can only carry so much load, analogous to the wing root bending moment and spar size problem. Further, the feathers of birds cannot carry heavy loads near the tip as demanded by elliptical spanloads, but a bell-shaped spanload has very light loads near the tip. And if the roll control of the bird is near the tips, the bird would not have adverse yaw. All of these solutions for the Hortens can be solved the same way as with birds.

The result of this is to see that the Wrights created flight by reducing the flight of birds to their component parts and solving each problem individually. The Hortens reintegrated the flight of birds into a single holistic unit that is optimal in all ways. Just as birds are.

This great revolutionary idea is one whose time has come. It is not recognized, even by some of today's foremost authorities in aeronautical engineering.

The story presented in this book is a snapshot of the creation during World War Two of one of the Hortens' most ambitious and beautiful aircraft, the Ho 229. It did not incorporate all the pieces necessary to solve the problems of the flight of birds. Yet the story is both compelling and beautiful, drawing us into the thoughts and ideas of the Hortens. Our thanks to Andrei Shepelev and Huib Ottens in weaving this tale together for us to enjoy, a tale of one of the truly beautiful, great and revolutionary ideas.

Al Bowers

Albion H. Bowers
Deputy Director of Research
NASA Dryden Flight Research Center
Edwards, California
31 March 2006

THE WING is the essential of flight, its means and its metaphor. Any other part that does not lift the aircraft pulls it down by its weight and drag. So if you want a better aircraft, why not dispense with fuselage and tail to leave *only the wing* – a flying wing?

This concept is as old as aviation itself – it can be traced down to the forerunners of the Wright brothers. However it took another pair of brothers to bring the idea to its most uncompromising realisation – the Horten brothers of Germany. Their line of beautiful all-wing aircraft culminated in the H IX (Ho 229) jet fighter-bomber. Coming too late to enter the battles of the Second World War, this amazing aircraft has nevertheless become renowned in the history of aeronautics.

Built from scrap materials in country workshops, carrying massive armour and heavy weaponry, able to operate from unpaved airstrips, able to withstand air combat and dive-bombing at 7g, able to deliver a one-ton bombload to targets 1,000 km away within one hour – while remaining invisible to radar… The Ho 229 *could* indeed have been a real '*Wunderwaffe*' … But did the Horten aircraft actually possess their claimed virtues? This book is an attempt to give an unbiased insight into the facts pertaining to one of the most extraordinary family of aircraft ever flown.

The longitudinal static stability of an aircraft without a horizontal tail is achieved through the use of self-stabilizing reflexed airfoils, or a swept wing with a negative geometric and/or aerodynamic twist (washout). Various design combinations of both reflexed airfoil and twist are possible. The upward-bent trailing edge of the reflexed-airfoil wing and the outer sections of the twisted and swept wing are analogous to a tail in that they create, in a level flight, a nose-up balancing force to trim the nose-down momentum of the lift force of the wing.

Since the arm of the trimming forces on a tailless aircraft is considerably less than that of a conventional tail, a greater downward force must be generated to reach an equal margin of static stability, thus reducing the total lift. For tailless aircraft, this results in a reduction of the lift coefficient by a factor of around one and a half compared to a conventional aircraft. On the other hand, the flying wing promises only half the drag coefficient of a conventional aircraft, so, in theory, the lift-to-drag ratio is better for the all-wing by a factor of 1,3. The American flying wing pioneer, John Knudsen Northrop, believed that the power required to propel a flying wing at the same speed as a conventional aircraft could be reduced by as much as 40 per cent and the range increased by 66 per cent.

The first practical tailless aircraft were created by the British designer J.W. Dunne between 1907 and 1919. His research established the fundamental principles of wing sweep and twist, the importance of a forward centre-of-gravity (c/g), and introduced the 'elevons' or combined elevators and ailerons as primary tailless control surfaces. The other pioneering contribution that influenced the Horten brothers was the 1910 Junkers patent for placing all aircraft components and loads inside the wing in order to reduce drag and the wing-root bending moment – the concept also known as 'spanloader'.[1]

Brothers Walter and Reimar Horten became involved in aircraft model building in 1925 at the ages of respectively only 12 and 10 years. Around 1927 they attended the courses in building flying models and strength and stress calculations held by their neighbour, Franz Wilhelm Schmitz. He was a teacher at the local trade school and a former engineer at the Junkers Flugzeugwerke A.G. His experience included the wind-tunnel testing and he thus was aware of the Junkers spanloader concept, first realised in the giant Junkers G 38 of the late 1920s. He became a close friend of the Horten family and often visited them to play the family piano. F.W. Schmitz influenced the younger Horten's conclusion that '…the flying wing is the aircraft of the future.'

In 1927 the Horten brothers started flying in primary gliders at the Bonn young fliers club and in the following years helped the Bonn '*Jungfliegergruppe*' at the Wasserkuppe. This mountain peak near Gersfeld in the Rhön Mountains, about 100 km north-east of Frankfurt, was, in the 1920s and 1930s, a German soaring 'Mecca', where the National gliding contest was held annually.

At the Wasserkuppe the Horten brothers witnessed flight of the tailless '*Storch*', designed by the then already well known aerodynamicist and aircraft designer, Alexander Lippisch. This sailplane, together with the Junkers' spanloader concept, would lead to the conception of the Hortens' *Nurflügel* – the

The Essence of Flight

The Origins and Fundamentals of the Flying Wing

John William Dunne (left) whose research established the fundamental principles of wing sweep and twist, the importance of a forward centre-of-gravity (c/g), and introduced the 'elevons' or combined elevators and ailerons as primary tailless control surfaces. He is seen here with Commandant Felix, who flew a Dunne D.8 from Eastchurch to Villacoublay in stages on 11 and 12 August 1913, thereby making the first tailless aircraft crossing of the English Channel.

Above: The British Dunne D.5 biplane at Eastchurch, 1910. The aircraft was controlled solely by the elevons (elevators/ailerons) fitted to the upper wing; the biplane's vertical surfaces were not fitted with rudders.

Right: Sketch from the 1910 Junkers Patent which placed all aircraft components and loads inside the wing in order to reduce drag and wing-root bending. A concept known as 'spanloader'.

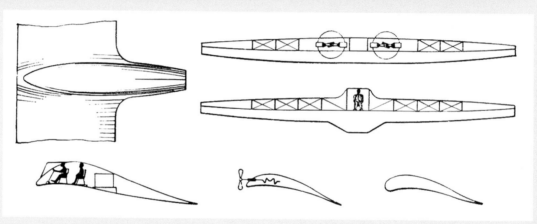

'only-wing' aircraft. During that time, the young brothers were creating for themselves a sound theoretical and practical basis from the building of their tailless model aircraft at home and testing them on the slopes of the nearby Venusberg and Rodderberg. By 1932, both brothers had earned their glider licences and started power flying. Still their combined flying experience was less than one hour.

The time had come for the brothers to think about building their own manned aircraft, as the more practical Walter urged the 'theoretician' Reimar: "*Do you want to do research or fly?*"

More importantly, a man-carrying aircraft would offer possibilities for experimentation that had not been available with models, such as control of the flight path and landing.

CHAPTER ONE

Fledged in the Third Reich

THE HORTEN brothers' venture into aircraft construction in pre-war Germany started at virtually the same moment the Nazi regime was established – sharing exactly the twelve year lifespan of the 'Thousand Year Reich'. When Adolf Hitler seized power on 30 January 1933, one of his first moves was to investigate teachers with a view to driving Jews out of German schools. When their school was temporarily closed, Reimar and Walter Horten took advantage of the unexpected holidays to commence the design and construction of their first full-size all-wing sailplane Horten I (H I). Parts of the aircraft were made at their parents' house at Venusbergweg 12 in Bonn and assembled in a hangar at Bonn-Hangelar airfield.

So as to leave no doubt about Alexander Lippisch's influence on their design, and as a mark of the admiration in which the young brothers held him, the H I was named *'Hangwind'* after Lippisch's nickname. Lippisch sometimes signed his articles on tailless aircraft developments, which were widely published in periodicals such as *Flugsport,* using this nickname. No wonder that the basic philosophy behind the H I was the

same as that of the Lippisch Delta series of tailless aircraft of the early 1930s. The arrow-shaped wings of the earlier Lippisch *Storch* series of aircraft, with their swept back leading and trailing edges, had evolved into a triangular or *Delta* wing planform, with a swept leading edge and a straight trailing edge. The result of this geometry was a wing with a very deep chord at the junction with the fuselage. This allowed for a thick wing section that could be utilised for additional storage. The fuselage, in turn, could be made smaller to lessen the associated parasite drag.

Building on the same idea, the H I design went further than that of the designer it was named after, paving the way for all subsequent Horten pure flying wing types with no fuselage and no vertical tail. The wing root of the H I was made thick enough to accommodate most of the pilot's body, with his head under the canopy protruding some 30 cm above the upper

The design work of Alexander Lippisch (left) greatly influenced the Horten brothers' early designs and their first full-size all-wing sailplane, the Horten I, was named 'Hangwind' after Lippisch's nickname. Lippisch is seen here relaxing with Hermann Köhl who made the first flight across the Atlantic from east to west in April 1928.

— The Horten Brothers —

*Oberleutnant Reimar Horten (left) is seen here in 1945, shortly before meeting Hermann Göring at Karinhall. **Walter Horten** (right) is seen here as an Oberleutnant in 1944, wearing the ribbon of the Iron Cross Second Class.*

REIMAR AND WALTER HORTEN were born on 12 March 1915 and 13 November 1913 respectively into the family of Max Horten, Professor of Philology, Theology and Philosophy at the University of Bonn, and his wife Elizabeth who had studied English Geography at Oxford. They had an older brother, Wolfram, and a younger sister, Gunilde. The children grew up in a very open minded and close family and were free to follow their own dreams and ambitions.

The youth of Reimar and Walter coincided with the time that German aviation rose from the ashes of the First World War. Due to the limitations on motorized flying as dictated by the Treaty of Versailles, the model building and sailplane movement flourished. Both Reimar and Walter became active members at a very early age. There they learned the principles of flight, design, aerodynamics and construction which formed the foundation for their future venture into the world of aircraft manufacturing. They learned to fly at the Bonn young fliers club in 1927.

Inspired by the tailless aircraft designs of Alexander Lippisch and the Junkers spanloader concept, the Horten brothers were convinced that the 'pure' flying wing was the shape of future aircraft.

From then on the Horten brothers designed and built a line of flying wing aircraft ranging from the Horten H I of 1933, the first attempt at a flying wing sailplane, to the Horten H IX (Ho 229) twin jet fighter-bomber of 1945. During this time Reimar and Walter worked closely together employing their personal talents and taking all the opportunities offered to them by the Third Reich, which was very positively inclined towards all things connected with aviation.

Reimar Horten was a genius of aerodynamics, possessed by the idea of the flying wing and willing to sacrifice almost everything to pursue his dreams. He was always working on new ideas or problems, using his indispensable slide-rule to make the necessary calculations.

Walter Horten was a very outgoing and easy man with an organisational talent and a flair for contacting the right people. He was also an excellent pilot who carried out many test flights in the Horten aircraft.

Reimar Horten died on 14 August 1993. Walter Horten died on 9 December 1998.

cables and push-rods to the control column. For directional control, drag rudders near the wingtips were introduced instead of the conventional fin-and-rudder arrangement, a novel feature never tried before. The rudder pedals could be pushed together for the drag rudders to act as spoilers – another device to be used on all later Horten aircraft. The wing loading was very low at 10 Kg/m^2.

Flight-tests in the mid-summer of 1933 at Bonn-Hangelar airfield advanced gradually from bungee-cord tows, through the car- and winch tows to aerotow launches. This cautious approach was necessary to investigate the aircraft's unusual stability and control characteristics. Unfortunately, these proved nearly as abnormal as the H I's appearance. Longitudinal balance would change with every movement of the elevator, to the point of pitch control reversal. Lateral control by ailerons did not work until their size and up travel was increased. Contrary to this, application of the drag rudder produced both yaw and bank, rendering the ailerons unnecessary for turning the aircraft. Yet, it would turn endlessly due to its indifferent directional stability, unless the opposite rudder was applied. A single-section rudder had been incorporated in the original design, located on the lower surface of the leading edge. This configuration caused a nose-down pitching moment; when an upper surface rudder section was added later, the directional control had to be spring-loaded to lessen its excessive air-braking action.

The longitudinal stability was eventually improved by moving the centre of gravity forward by means of lead ballast, but remained sensitive to changes in c/g location. In one case the H I crash-landed when Reimar Horten flew it trimmed for the heavier Walter.

The Hortens considered the problem of longitudinal stability as solved already with their first full-size aircraft, the H 1. It was established that c/g must be located as far forward as possible for the tailless aircraft to have acceptable handling characteristics. However, because of the short moment arm in pitch of the flying wing, the c/g travel must be kept within very close limits, which could pose difficulties in operation.

By March 1934 only about two hours' flying time on the H I had been added by the brothers to their modest flying experience. Nonetheless the remarkable flying wing did attract the attention of the local branch of the National Aero Club, which welcomed it to the flying meeting held at Bonn-Hangelar in June. Reimar was granted free aerotows and finally got an airworthiness permit for the H I (coded 'D-*Hangwind*'), despite the fact that he had performed another hard landing in the face of the airworthiness authorities. Now the way was clear to the Wasserkuppe.

By that time Walter had joined the newly created German *Wehrmacht*, and Reimar was still at school while the first week of the Rhön contest passed by. It was not before the end of the week that Walter

wing surface; a keel structure below contained the seat and a rubber-mounted skid. The deep wing root tapered off to the wingtips, creating a triangular wing with an almost straight trailing edge; the wing section was symmetrical with 20 per cent of chord thickness. The airframe was made entirely of wood; the wing nose was covered with thin model-building plywood. The rest of the aircraft was skinned with linen. Conventional ailerons and elevators occupied the full length of the trailing edge, linked through

The H I 'D-Hangwind' glider inside the First World War vintage hangar at Bonn-Hangelar airfield. The placards hanging on the wooden-plank walls recall prominent events in the airfield's past.

The H I 'D-Hangwind' being prepared for air-towing under supervision of the airfield police.

The Horten brothers with their first glider. As far as it can be made out, Walter is sitting in the cockpit while Reimar is standing in front of the aircraft.

Hitlerjugend members posing proudly beside the H1 'D-Hangwind'.

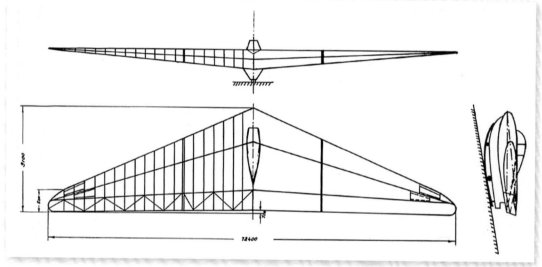

Three-view line drawing of the H1 'Hangwind'.

aerotowed the H I with Reimar at the controls to the *'Kuppe'* during a spell of bad weather. During the landing the glider was damaged, and the ensuing repair was finished just two days before the contest ended. Since Walter had returned to his regiment and there was no way of transporting the *'Hangwind'* back home, Reimar telephoned Alexander Lippisch, who was at the time in Darmstadt as chief of the Technical department of the *Deutsche Forschungsanstalt für Segelflug* (DFS), and offered him the H I for free. Lippisch declined the offer, leaving Reimar with no choice but to burn the glider on site. Reimar Horten recalled later: *"We didn't want anyone to be harmed by the bad characteristics of the H I. That's why we destroyed it and would not allow other pilots to fly it."* [2]

It is interesting to note that the same bad characteristics had been peculiar to Lippisch's *'Delta I'* which was similar to the H I in general arrangement and control layout. Though not taking any place in the competition, the Horten wing won a prize of 600 *Reichsmarks* for design originality – thus at least paying off the 320 *Reichsmarks* spent on its construction. The total flying time of the H I, of which the construction had taken nearly 1,000

hours, was only about seven hours, of which Reimar had undertaken less than one hour. Nevertheless, the brothers' 'first-born' had flown, and it was an aircraft akin to none.

The second Horten design, the H II *'Habicht'* ('Hawk'), was to prove much more successful. The concept of the follow-on for the advanced but troubled H I began around the early autumn of 1933, shortly after the first flights of the *'Hangwind'*. Aside from the stability and control issues, the Hortens planned to resolve the problem of towing by making the H II a motorglider. Construction began around the summer of the following year, again in the Horten family house in Bonn.

Fortunately for the young Horten brothers, they were not alone in grappling with the fundamental problems of tailless aircraft design. Around the time the H II was being conceived, the Hortens' guru, Alexander Lippisch, published a work which proved very useful in answering some of Reimar's questions. Included in it was a method of calculation for an optimal wing design based on the 'lifting line' theory of Professor Dr.-Ing. Ludwig Prandtl. Reimar attended lectures that Lippisch gave during his visits to Bonn University and wrote letters to Lippisch and Prandtl asking for advice and exchanging his ideas. Early in 1935, Reimar went to Bonn University to take classes in mathematics.

According to Reimar Horten's later statements,[3] he first introduced the 'bell-shaped lift distribution' (BSLD) to the aerodynamic design of the H II. He had no access to a wind tunnel to prove his ideas experimentally, so the only way to progress was to build an aircraft and fly it. After all, that was the way that Lippisch had conducted his research.

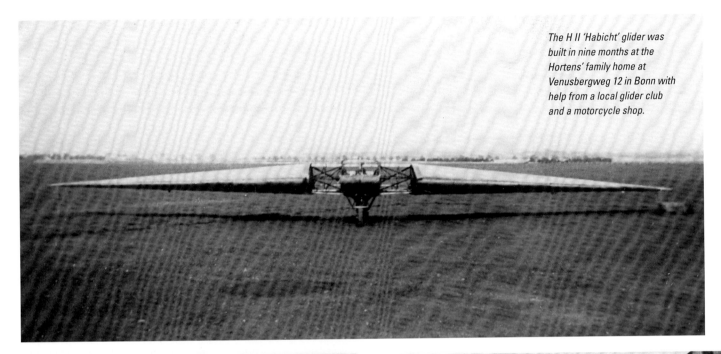

The H II 'Habicht' glider was
built in nine months at the
Hortens' family home at
Venusbergweg 12 in Bonn with
help from a local glider club
and a motorcycle shop.

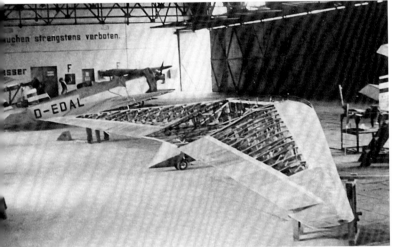

The finished H II 'Habicht' sitting
before the hangar at Bonn-
Hangelar airfield.

Above left: Final assembly of the
H II 'Habicht' glider in a hangar
at the Bonn-Hangelar airfield.

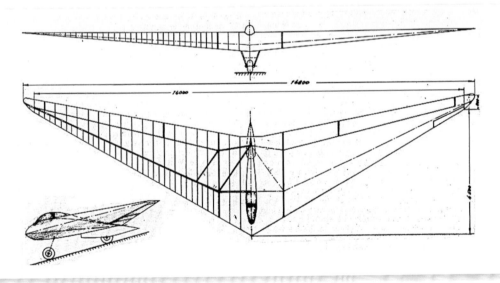

A three-view line drawing of the
H II L.

As a first step, the H I wing profiles were reportedly modified in December 1933. It was probably at that stage that its wing received a strong non-linear negative twist of 7 degrees, with most of the washout located at the last quarter of the half span.

For the wing root section of the H II, a reflexed camber-line airfoil was adopted of the 'constant centre of pressure' type developed by the *Aerodynamische Versuchsanstalt* (Aerodynamic Test Institute, AVA) in Göttingen. This profile blended into a symmetrical airfoil at the wing tips.

The H IIm is towed to its start position.

Right: The H IIm seen during take-off.

The H IIm seen during its landing approach.

Above right: Details of the Hirth HM 60R motor and propeller extension shaft of the H IIm. The fixed-pitch two-blade propeller was handmade by Peter Kümpel from beech wood.
Test-flying ended after the borrowed engine had to be returned to its owner.

This layout was to become standard for all subsequent Horten aircraft, along with the wooden outer wing panels with a D-nose spar, attached to a centre section steel-tube framework. The lateral and longitudinal controls were combined in elevons, the inboard elevators replaced by landing flaps. Despite the fact that the BSLD was supposed to make possible the 'single control' system for a tailless aircraft, both the H II and all the following wartime Horten types did have brake rudders for directional control.

The wingspan, sweepback and twist had been increased on the H II, compared to the H I, and the trailing edge had been made swept. The tandem-type undercarriage had brakes, a steerable tailwheel and a retractable front wheel.

A most unusual feature of the Horten II was that the pilot seating was arranged in a supine position to reduce the drag to the very minimum. Construction of the H II had taken 5,000 hours, five times more than the H I. The aircraft made its maiden flight in May 1935. Later the glider was

fitted with a 79 hp Hirth HM 60R piston engine, mounted inside the centre section close to c/g and driving a pusher propeller through an extension shaft, to become the H IIm motor glider.

By the time the H II was test flown, new Horten projects were already in the works. The H III and IV sailplanes failed to interest the aircraft industry and were set aside, while the H V twin-pusher two-seater did attract the attention of the chemical company Dynamit AG at Troisdorf near Köln.

The H V was proposed in response to the interest expressed by the *Reichsluftfahrtministerium* (RLM, Reich Air Ministry) for an aircraft of tailless configuration, which could provide an unobstructed rear view for aerial surveillance and a rear-firing defensive gun. Aircraft of this kind had been created before in Great Britain, such as the Westland-Hill 'Pterodactyl' series of 1928-1934, and in Russia, such as the Kalinin K-12 of 1936. In Germany in 1935 the Gothaer Waggonfabrik had built and tested the Gotha Go 147 parasol monoplane which

Span-Wise Lift Distribution

In the early 20th century Prof. Dr.-Ing. Ludwig Prandtl at the University of Göttingen discovered the phenomenon of induced drag, which is a drag created by a lifting wing due to the difference in pressure between the lower and upper surfaces of the wing. This pressure differential causes a flow across the wingtip, which couples with inflow to develop a vortex. The energy wasted for the creation of this vortex manifests itself as drag.

In 1918, Prandtl published his wing theory which established an elliptical lift distribution (ELD) across the wingspan (or elliptical spanload) as one developing the least possible induced drag for a given wingspan.

In 1933, he proposed another (approximate) solution to the span-wise lift distribution, which offered a still lower induced drag compared to ELD — but only for an unconstrained wingspan. The wingspan was taken as variable this time, while the net lift and associated wing root bending moment were taken as constants. The resultant curve had the shallow depressions towards the low-loaded wingtips. In theory, this lift distribution offered less induced drag at the expense of a longer wingspan. In a sense, the 'additional' outboard sections of the bell-shape-loaded wing can be viewed as precursors to modern-day winglets.

It can be observed that despite the same wing root bending moment, the longer wingspan would nevertheless result in an extra structural weight and a greater parasite drag. The question whether this could be justified by a decrease in induced drag, is a subject of an actual design optimisation. This solution might be favourable for sailplanes, soaring slowly at high lift coefficients (C_L), where the wingtip vortices generate the major part of the overall drag.

Due to the shape of the distribution curve it was later termed the 'bell-shaped lift distribution' (BSLD, or Glocken-Auftriebs-Verteilung, GAV, in German) by Reimar Horten.

Adverse Yaw

This Prandtl solution for the minimum induced drag was not aimed specifically at tailless aircraft or flying wings. Moreover, there have been serious doubts expressed whether the Hortens were aware of this theory at the time.[4] What was of importance to Reimar, was that the low loading on the outboard wing area, which the BSLD offered, could minimise the effect of adverse yaw encountered by the Hortens with the H I.

The adverse yaw is the effect whereby the aircraft turns in a direction opposite to its bank. This effect is a product of the lift-induced drag. During a turn, the wing the pilot induces to rise increases the lift. This also increases the induced drag, which drags the up-moving wing aft, opposite to the desired yaw direction. In a conventional aircraft, a vertical tail and rudder serve to counteract the adverse yaw.

With the outboard wing loading close to zero in a bell-shaped distribution, the aileron deflections will cause a near symmetrical drag increase on both wingtips, hence no yawing moment. Then if the outboard loading is negative, one can expect a reversal of the adverse yaw into pro-verse yaw, so the aircraft would turn in the direction it banks. (Reimar even put forth a theory of 'negative drag' or 'wingtip thrust' due to the BSLD). In this way it would be possible to turn the aircraft with elevons alone without the need for a rudder; since the elevons are used also for the pitch control, they would constitute the 'single control' system. In fact Reimar recognised the BSLD as producing a greater induced drag, compared to the elliptical lift distribution (ELD) wing with the same span, but he was ready to accept this disadvantage in order to obtain the desired flight behaviour.

There is no hard evidence, however, whether the Hortens had completely solved the adverse yaw problem. It seems they did not, or at least not until 1955. One possible reason for this is that the calculation method they used did not take into account the effect of the wing sweep. A paper on this subject had been published by Dipl.-Ing. Hans Multhopp as a secret document published in 1938 [5], but was not used by Reimar at the time.

Reports indicate that the Horten wings had to be turned mainly by the drag rudders, as these rotated the aircraft around both the roll and yaw axis. In this way, stable coordinated turns could be easily made and this was ideal for circling in thermals.

Wing Twist

A straightforward way to obtain the ELD is to give the wing an elliptical planform. Such a wing is rarely seen on aircraft (the Supermarine Spitfire is one of the few examples) because of the technological limitations. A conventional tapered wing with straight edges is easier to build; to give it the needed lift distribution one can twist the wing along the span.

Since a typical swept-wing tailless design does already envisage some washout for stability reasons, it is natural to adapt this washout to achieve an optimal spanload as well. A simple linear wing twist, whereby the angle of incidence increases evenly towards the wingtips, will give an approximation for the ELD. For the BSLD, a non-linear distribution of the wing twist is required. Therefore, any wing with such a twist will have the BSLD — but only for one given angle of attack.

Stall Behaviour

As an additional bonus the wing twist improves the stall behaviour of the wing at high angles of attack, since separation of the airflow occurs first at the root sections of the wing. This leaves the outer parts of the wings at a lower local angle of attack, with the ailerons (elevons) remaining fully effective. This is why the wing twist is widely used on wings of conventional aircraft.

Mitten-Effekt

During the trials of the H II the Hortens found that the centre section of the swept-wing was producing much less lift than anticipated, so the lift distribution deviated from the one calculated and the aircraft became nose heavy. This problem was called the 'Mitten-Effekt' ('middle effect') by the Hortens and influenced all their subsequent designs. The initial approach to solve the problem was the adoption of a parabola-shaped planform for the wing leading edge, having the local sweep angles gradually reducing to zero at the centreline. In 1938 the Hortens built a small 'Parabel' glider (photo at left) to test this concept. This aircraft was damaged in an accident and it never flew. However, such a wing shape was considered impracticable, so for the H V the Hortens adopted a simpler iteration of the parabola-wing that incorporated a step in the sweepback of the leading edge.

However, the real cause of this phenomena lies in the fact that until the late 1940s there was no method to determine the lift distribution of a swept-wing; calculations were being made based on an assumption of a straight wing with the same measurements. This approach gave inadequate results because the lift characteristics of a swept-wing are different from those of a straight wing.

strongly resembled Geoffrey Hill's Pterodactyl V. The Hortens' proposal was for a much more streamlined all-wing design powered by two Hirth HM 60R engines. The field of fire for a rear gun was to be provided between the two contra-rotating pusher propellers.

For Dynamit AG the objective of the project was to try aircraft construction applications for its newest phenol-based composite materials. The company's synthetic materials 'Mipolan' and 'Astralon' had previously been used for the production of various curved parts of the H II, and had performed well, so the new design was to try a still wider utilisation of these early plastics.

At that time Walter was training as a pilot on the Dornier Do 23 with *Kampfgeschwader* 155 at Giebelstadt near Würzburg. To fly this sluggish bomber was a disappointment for Walter, for he wanted to become a fighter pilot and he wanted to help Reimar with his H V project at Troisdorf. Walter approached *Generalleutnant* Walter Wever, the *Luftwaffe* Chief of Staff, asking for a transfer to a garrison close to Köln so that he could help his brother after his regular duty hours. Photographs of the Hortens' unusual *Nurflügel* did help to attract Wever's interest, and so in May 1936, Walter was transferred to the third Gruppe of the newly created *Jagdgeschwader* 134 'Horst Wessel' fighter wing, III./JG 134, based at Lippstadt, 110 km north-east of Köln. Soon Walter would have a very busy time training on Arado Ar 65/68 fighters, and visiting Troisdorf whenever possible to help Reimar.

To test the revolutionary plastic technology, the Hortens built from the new materials two wing sets for a primary glider named *'Hol's der Teufel'* (or 'devil may catch it', a curse or oath if one was to hit one's finger with a hammer rather than hitting the nail's head), which resulted in a 15 per cent reduction in weight over the original. Following

flight-tests in May 1936, one wing was statically loaded to destruction, and the other endured a weather test for six months in the open air. A multitude of other tests concerning material strength and construction technology had been carried out for the H V project.

The work at Troisdorf was soon interrupted however, when Reimar was called up for military service. Fortunately for the Horten brothers, Walter's *Gruppenkommandeur* in JG 134 was *Hauptmann* Oskar Dinort, who had been a well-known glider pilot and a Horten acquaintance since the Wasserkuppe. Dinort made Reimar a reserve officer in JG 134, where he was given basic training and later assigned to duties as a flight instructor. Before long, Dinort proposed that Reimar build three additional H II's, one each for him, Reimar and Walter to take part in the forthcoming 1937 Rhön contest. At Reimar's disposal were the Lippstadt workshops, necessary materials and labour, paid for by the *Luftwaffe* via Dinort. Reimar was relieved of most of his military duties, so he was able to improve the original H II design. The airframe was strengthened to make the glider capable of aerobatics and allow for the installation of Hirth engines that Dinort promised to supply. In the new H II 'L' version, the pilot's prone position was abandoned because of the poor visibility from the cockpit to both sides and when flying at high angles of attack, when the pilot's feet would be higher than his head.

At the same time, the work on the H V continued at Troisdorf. It was intended to improve the slow flight characteristics with more effective flaps. The increased nose-down momentum of deployed flaps was to be trimmed by elevons in the form of wingtips rotating about skewed hinges, arranged so that they increased incidence while rotating forward, and vice versa. This so-called 'waggle-tip' system should also have provided the desired

Oskar Dinort signals that he is ready to take off in his flimsy glider during a glider meeting in 1924. Dinort later went on to become a Generalmajor in the Luftwaffe and was awarded the Ritterkreuz with Oakleaves in July 1941 for his services as Gruppenkommandeur of I./St.G 2 'Immelmann'. He flew more than 150 combat missions and ended the war as Kommodore of 3. Fliegerschuldivision.

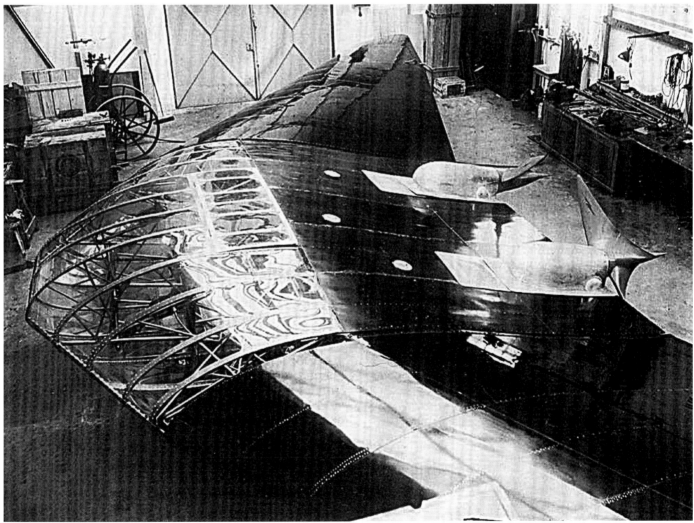

Construction of the H Va using synthetic materials like Trolitax, Mipolan and Astralon. The nose-section, housing the crew of two prone pilots, was covered with Cellon transparent film. The unusually shaped wooden props were coated with Lignofol.

The H Va and the H IIm at Bonn-Hangelar airfield.

Another view of the H Va at Bonn-Hangelar.

The large spats covering the fixed main undercarriage legs were supposed to improve directional stability of the H Va.

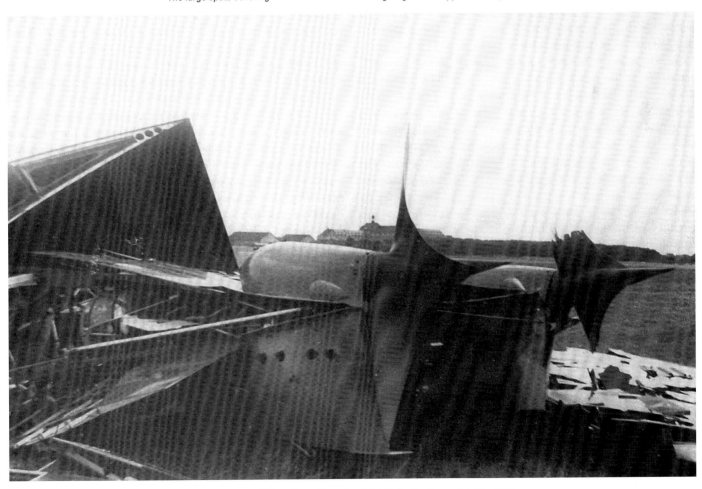

The wreckage of the H Va at Bonn-Hangelar airfield following its crash in May 1937.

> **Landing the Flying Wing**
>
> *In general, deployment of landing flaps produces a nose-down momentum that must be counteracted by upward deflection of longitudinal control surfaces, which action reduces total lift. The shorter moment arm of the longitudinal controls of a flying wing, as compared to those of a conventional aircraft, requires greater trimming forces which result in greater loss of total lift in the landing configuration. This is partly offset by the ability of the swept flying wings to perform landings at higher angles of attack, and their generally lower wing loading.*
>
> *There was also a ground effect encountered during the landings of the later versions of the H V, whereby its deep wing, coupled with extended flaps, generated a kind of dynamic air cushion. This prevented a hard landing, but also delayed the touchdown, causing the aircraft to 'float' along the runway.*

Both the D-10-125 and the second H II L, D-10-131, wore the same white-red-black paint scheme.

simultaneous bank and yaw control with no need for a rudder.

The contra-rotating fixed pitch propellers of the H V were installed directly on the crankshafts of its engines, which were mounted at the extreme aft of the centre section. This layout left stability at its margin with the c/g at the aft limit. The H V crashed during its first flight in May 1937 at Bonn-Hangelar. One engine cut out following a bounce on take-off and the aircraft flipped over a wingtip (According to

Reimar the power loss was caused by mishandling of the throttles by Walter). Both Reimar and Walter were injured in the crash. The unique variable-geometry flying wing was shattered beyond repair; its plastic panels with paper used as a matrix proved too fragile. The H V had cost Dynamit AG 40,000 *Reichsmarks*, but yielded the company valuable know-how and several patents. The 'plastic flying wing' also brought the Horten brothers their first publicity within the *Luftwaffe*.

Meanwhile the first H II L, registered D-10-125, was finished by June 1937, followed soon by the second D-10-131 just in time for both to take part in the 1937 Rhön contest. Neither of the H II L's performed well in the competition due to excessive nose-heaviness, insufficient pilot training and lack of a retrieval crew. Reimar crash-landed his H II L several times, prompting the chief of the Rhön contest to report to Dinort that the Horten wing was in no condition to compete. Completion of the third H II L, D-11-187 (D-13-387), was delayed until 1938 because of the re-militarisation of the Rhineland.

By that time III./JG 134 had been reorganised in late March 1937 into II./LG *'Greifswald'* equipped with Messerschmitt Bf 109B/Ds. The new commander did not like the Hortens' work, but before Dinort left the *Lehrgeschwader* in late August 1937, he informed the *General-luftzeugmeister* (GL Chief of Technical Department of the RLM) *Generaloberst* Ernst Udet, about the brothers. The Hortens managed to establish a close relationship with Udet, whose aerobatics they had admired at the 1931-32 airshows at Bonn-Hangelar, and who subsequently became their new protector. Udet transferred the brothers to Ostheim airfield near Köln, the new base of JG 26 *'Schlageter'*. Here the work on the H II L gliders continued, and a new version of the H V was started using conventional construction methods.

Since one of the causes of the H V crash was thought to be the problematic reclined position of its pilots, the new H Vb was redesigned with two separate canopies allowing for a normal seating position. The wingspan was enlarged by two metres and the rotating wingtips were replaced with conventional elevons.[6] The Hirth engines, which had survived the H V crash, were used again, this time installed close to the c/g, driving the props via V-belts and overhead extension shafts. The undercarriage was a fixed tricycle (the

H IIIc (D-12-347) and the H IIIa (D-12-348) at Wasserkuppe. Both gliders were lost on 6 August 1938.

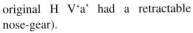

original H V'a' had a retractable nose-gear).

Following the completion of the last H II L and in parallel to the H Vb work, the Hortens started a new glider project, ordered in 1937 by Dinort for the 1938 Rhön contest. The new H III was basically an enlarged H II L with a 20.4 m wingspan and a shortened root-chord resulting in an increased aspect ratio. The double elevons were introduced deflecting at differentiated angles in order to retain washout. Based on previous experience with the H II, the control linkage was mounted on ball bearings to overcome the friction problem. The fixed undercarriage was of the tandem-wheel type.

As a possible solution for the 'Mitten-Effekt' problem, a parabolic leading edge for the centre section was first considered, and then dropped in favour of a small foreplane above the forward centre section. This was adopted on the H IIIc (D-12-347), first flown on 7 May 1938. The H IIIa (D-12-348) was similar to the 'c' model, but missed the foreplane; it was completed in the summer of 1938

One of the 'series' H IIIbs,
D-4-683, built in Berlin in 1939.

The famous aviatrix Hanna
Reitsch inspects a Horten glider
together with "Rhönvater"
Oskar Ursinus. Hanna Reitsch
tested a H IIL in 1938 and was
particularly pleased with the
stall characteristics of the
flying wing.

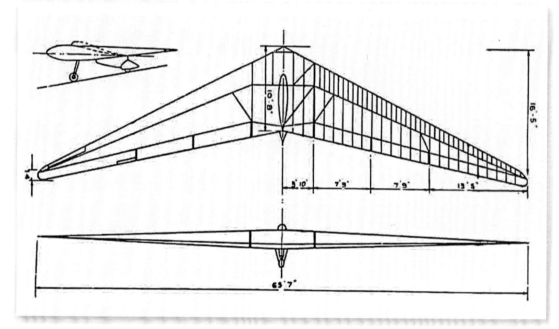

A three-view line drawing of
the H III.

just in time for the Rhön contest. Both gliders were lost at the Rhön competition on 6 August after flying into a thunderstorm and reaching an incredible altitude of over 7,500 m. The H IIIc pilot, Werner Blech, lost his life in the accident, while the second pilot, Heinz Scheidhauer, suffered from severe frostbite, but survived. After being hospitalised for six months Scheidhauer remained with the Hortens for many years to come as their test-pilot, flying almost all of their flying wing designs. The overall performance demonstrated by the Horten gliders, however, convinced the RLM to order ten examples of the 'series' H IIIb, officially designated the 8-250.[7]

Later that year the H Vb was demonstrated in Berlin to RLM officials, but no contract was awarded.[8] Around this time, Udet requested Hanna Reitsch to test a Horten aircraft. The famous aviatrix

was a research and test pilot at the DFS where she tested, among others, the latest designs by Lippisch. Reitsch flew the H II L (D-11-187) in November 1938. Her report indicated good longitudinal stability and control, but unsatisfactory lateral and directional control and bad control harmonisation. Stall characteristics were excellent, as the aircraft could not "…by any sort of control movements be made to drop the wing or to "spin"." This particular aircraft was lost in an accident in March of the following year; the other two remained most of the time at the Hortens' disposal for test purposes. The planned engines were never fitted to the gliders.

In 1938, the Horten brothers were awarded the Lilienthal Prize for their contribution to aeronautical advance. The same year Reimar was discharged from the Luftwaffe. Early in 1939, after the DFS Lippisch group had been engaged by Messerschmitt

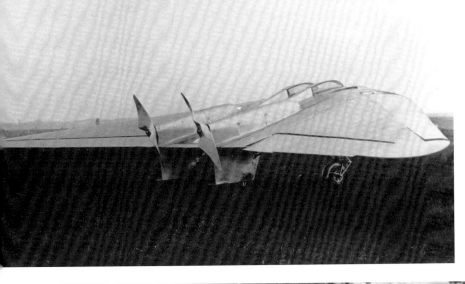

The Hirth engines of the H Vb were installed further forward than on the H Va, as evident from the longer engine fairings.

Above: JG 26 groundcrew inspect the H Vb at the Köln-Ostheim airfield. Note that the propellers are different from the H Va.

Details of the twin canopy and the fixed nose-landing gear of the H Vb. Both the H II L and the H Vb, modified with the sitting pilot's position, retained their transparent nose skinning to facilitate downward visibility.

AG for the development of a rocket-propelled tailless aircraft, Udet arranged for the Horten brothers to discuss a similar arrangement with *Dr.-Ing.* Ernst Heinkel. It was proposed to establish within the Heinkel Company a design office for tailless aircraft with Reimar in charge. Plans were laid out for building three prototypes of the H VII, an H V-based fighter-bomber which had originally been proposed in autumn 1938. The RLM was interested in this project, but negotiations were stopped after Heinkel claimed the patent rights for all existing and future Horten works.

Reimar himself did not pay much attention to patenting his ideas. In the event, this would not make any difference after the cancellation of the patent right in the Third Reich. Reimar later blamed Heinkel's chief designer, Heinrich Hertel, for the failure of the deal. Still, Reimar was less than certain whether he actually wanted to work within an established firm, or to go out on his own with all the inherent management worries, but free to create anything that he liked.

Then in 1939 Reimar chose to continue his education instead of hiring out to Heinkel. On Udet's order, his brother Walter went to study at the Technical University in Berlin-Charlottenburg. Their education was interrupted again when the Second World War broke out in September 1939.

CHAPTER TWO

Nurflügel goes to War

Wolfram Horten, Walter and Reimar's elder brother, who was killed during a mine-laying operation in the English Channel in May 1940.

WHEN Germany invaded Poland in September 1939, Walter and Reimar were called back to their earlier duties with the *Luftwaffe*. Their older brother Wolfram was to die on 20 May 1940 when his mine-laying Heinkel He 111 exploded over the sea near Dunkirk in France. As a maritime pilot Wolfram had inspired Reimar's next project, the long-range reconnaissance/strike H VIII intended to search for enemy shipping along the European coast. It was to be a double-sized H III powered by between four or six Junkers Jumo 210 engines, with a 24-hour endurance and capable of flying beyond England at 400 km/h with a two- or three-man crew.

Walter became a Technical Officer with I./JG 26, now under the command of *Major* Adolf Galland. He entered the air war on the Western Front, flying his Messerschmitt Bf 109E as Galland's wingman. Prior to an order released in September 1940 which forbade Technical Officers to fly combat operations, Walter claimed seven victories in the 45 missions he flew with Galland in the Battle of Britain. Although three of his 'kills' happened to be Supermarine Spitfires, Walter had realised only too well from his combat experiences

the advantages that the Spitfire's low wing-loading gave to its pilot. His respect for this fighter was only confirmed later when he test-flew a captured Spitfire V against a Focke-Wulf Fw 190. In addition, the Messerschmitts, both the Bf 109 fighter and the Bf 110 twin-engined *Zerstörer* ('destroyer' or heavy fighter), had been designed with a high wing-loading for high speed at low altitude, and performed poorly at high altitude. The Spitfire, which had originally been designed for a combat altitude of 7,000 metres, would usually bounce the Messerschmitts from high altitude. In a dogfight, the lower wing-loading again gave it the advantage of a tighter turning radius.

In the second half of 1940 Walter went to Braunschweig to discuss this problem with Reimar, who had been transferred to the glider pilot school there in late August 1940. Reimar, who by that time had also been trained as a Bf 109 pilot, showed Walter some drawings he had made of a fighter version of their recent H VII project. This twin-pusher could eventually replace the Bf 110s in the *Zerstörer* units which had lost their best pilots while protecting bombers during the Battle of Britain. The Hortens were confident that the inherent low wing-loading of the *Nurflügel* would provide it with superiority at all altitudes.

As the Battle of Britain raged on, all kinds of landing vehicles were being gathered at the French side of the English Channel in preparation for *Unternehmen Seelöwe* (Operation 'Sea Lion'), the planned invasion of the British Isles. Among these, five Horten H IIIbs and two H IILs were brought together at Braunschweig, along with eighty DFS *Kranich* sailplanes, to be modified as ammunition carriers for the *Fallschirmjäger* (air-assault) units. The two H IILs were later replaced by Reimar Horten with two H IIIbs taken from storage, in order to standardise the fleet of seven all-wing cargo gliders.

A 200 kg cargo pallet, the same load as carried by a *Kranich*, was installed in the centre section of the H IIIb and four more cargo compartments for 50 kg standard ammunition boxes were provided in the outer wings. The glider's gross weight was more than doubled without a substantial increase in the wing bending moments and so there was no need to strengthen the airframe, as the flying wing's payload was distributed evenly across its span.

By the year's end, it was becoming increasingly evident that the *Luftwaffe* was not able to achieve air superiority in British skies, so *Unternehmen Seelöwe* was cancelled. Reimar now had the time to return to one of his earlier projects, the H IV high-performance sailplane. A mock-up of its centre section had been started before the gliding school was transferred to Königsberg-Neuhausen in December 1940. At the new base in East Prussia, Reimar Horten had enough personnel under his command to finish his purely private H IV. It was test-flown by Heinz Scheidhauer in May 1941, shortly before the gliding school was moved again, this time to Frankfurt-am-Main.

With the H IV, Reimar was to explore the effect of aspect ratio, which was doubled when compared to the H III with the same span. The parabola geometry, as the solution to the 'Mitten Effekt', had been incorporated again, not to the leading edge but to the 'T-4' line through the maximum thickness points of the wing sections. (Ideally this line coincides with the quarter chord line, although on most of the Horten designs the location of the maximum thickness point of the airfoils varied from 30 per cent chord at the root to 20 per cent at the tips). Since the leading edge of the H IV had the simple straight-line sweep, the parabolic 'T-4' line led to a bend in the trailing edge that converged in a pointed bat-like tail.

The elevons were divided into three sections deflecting at differentiated angles in order to retain the effect of wing twist. Along with the usual drag rudders on the upper and lower wing surfaces, spoiler-type dive brakes were installed for glide path control. The outer wing panels had such thin sections that they had to be made of magnesium alloy to withstand the loads.

A prone position for the pilot was attempted again with the H IV. A glider with the pilot lying on his belly, such as in the Wright brothers' early designs, had been built by *Akaflieg Stuttgart* in 1939 for the purpose of investigating a pilot's endurance of high G-forces in this position. This aircraft inspired Reimar to design the H IV with a pilot

One of the seven H IIIb (Ho 250) cargo gliders prepared for participation in the planned invasion of the British Isles. The uppersurfaces are finished in standard 'broken' camouflage of Black Green/Dark Green RLM 70/71. The photograph to the left shows cargo stowed in the starboard wing.

Oblt. Walter Horten seen here during his time as Technical Officer of 1./JG 26. He flew 45 missions over England during the Battle of Britain, claiming seven victories. The Bf 109 E-7 in the background was flown by Hptm. Josef Priller, the Gruppenkommandeur of III./JG 26.

Heinz Scheidhauer worked with the Hortens for many years as their chief test-pilot, testing most of the Horten sailplane and light engined flying wings. He is seen here in the uniform of a Luftwaffe Feldwebel.

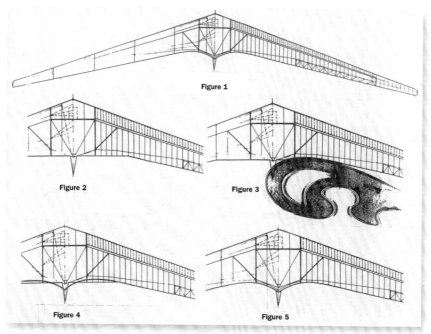

Figure 1

Figure 2

Figure 3

Figure 4

Figure 5

According to the recollections of Karl Nickel and Gunilde Nickel (born Horten), the prominent 'Horten-tail' shown here was invented by Walter Horten for "aesthetic reasons", the aerodynamic justification provided much later by Reimar. The original straight trailing edge (Figure 2) was smoothed out by Reimar after much discussion with a quadratic parabola (Figure 5). Schematic by courtesy of Karl Nickel.

The first H IV shows off a very high aspect ratio of its wing. The nosewheel is a detachable device used for ground handling.

Heini Dittmar, who flew the rocket-powered Messerschmitt Me 163 AV4, at Peenemünde on 13 August 1941.

accommodated in a semi-prone position. His spine was reclined at about 30 degrees, which resulted in a lesser strain on the pilot's neck. A small plastic bubble protruded above the wing to accommodate the pilot's head and upper body. His knees and lower legs were in a 'keel' below the wing, which also housed a spring suspended main skid. The retractable nose skid replaced the rather weak tandem wheel undercarriage of the H III, which had proven unsuitable for rough terrain landings. For take-off a jettisonable wheel was attached to the nose skid.

Although susceptible to wing flutter, the H IV belonged to the best gliders of its time. A comparison test in May 1941 demonstrated that the H IV was second only to the best German glider of that time, the Darmstadt D-30 *Cirrus*. The glider destined to become number one was called the

H VI, an uncompromised 32+ aspect ratio sailplane that was already in Reimar's plans and dreams, though far from realisation yet.

Meanwhile, Walter Horten was transferred in May 1941 from Brest in France to Berlin as Technical Advisor in the Technical Department of *Luftwaffe-Inspektion* 3, LIn 3, (the 3rd (Fighter) Inspectorate of the *Luftwaffe*). Initially his superior was Kurt-Bertram von Döring, who had been his *Geschwaderkommodore* in JG 134. Walter's assignment was to inspect the operational status of the fighter units. In the second half of that year, Walter performed these duties under the command of the *General der Jagdflieger* (General of Fighters) Werner Mölders, then from early 1942 under Adolf Galland.

Walter Horten's new position and connections brought the brothers an abundance of information on the newest developments in the aircraft industry, which appeared to firmly support their way of thinking. Firstly, research by aerodynamicist Adolf Busemann had shown the advantage of a swept-wing for reaching high transonic speeds. Secondly, a number of jet propulsion designs were being developed in Germany, promising unheard-of powers and aerodynamic efficiency of propeller-less powerplants – their compact configurations ideally merging with the streamlined flying wing.

In the autumn of 1941, Walter took Reimar to the Peenemünde test centre to witness one of the first powered flights of *Dr.* Lippisch's Me 163A tailless rocket fighter prototype. Flown by the famous glider pilot Heini Dittmar, this little aircraft attained speeds close to 900 km/h when taking off from the ground under its own power. On 2 October 1941, starting the rocket motor in the air after being towed to altitude, Dittmar for the first time reached the 1,000 km/h mark. Reimar was surprised to learn that the fastest aircraft in the world had wings made entirely of wood, just like the Horten gliders. It was encouraging news for the Hortens, despite the fact that their opponent was way ahead with his different

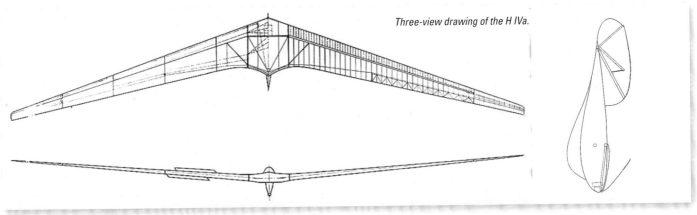

Three-view drawing of the H IVa.

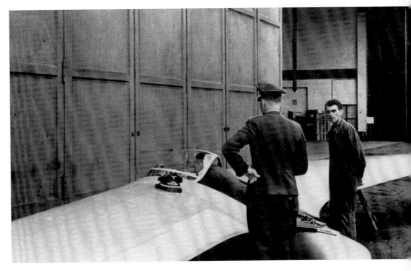

tailless philosophy. Apparently, they had little chance of beating the speed of Lippisch's diminutive aircraft, designed with the least possible parasite drag in mind. Instead, the Hortens' 'pure' flying wing was supposed to have the best lift-to-drag ratio, which was favourable for a longer-range aircraft.

Fortunately for the Hortens, they very soon had the opportunity to further their all-wing fighter project. After several attempts, they succeeded in obtaining Udet's approval for modifying their H Vb as a single-seat H Vc. Since the beginning of the war, the H Vb had been left in the open at Potsdam-Werder airfield and consequently had been seriously damaged by the elements. A repair contract was awarded to Peschke Flugzeugbau in Minden. Otto Peschke had been a fighter pilot during the

First World War. His company, formerly a furniture manufacturer, was busy repairing light aircraft and manufacturing ailerons for the Fw 190, using mostly forced labourers from France, Poland, Denmark and the occupied regions of the Soviet Union. The Horten brothers had become acquainted with Peschke at Bonn-Hangelar where he served in 1927-1928 as an instructor of the local flying school. To oversee the reconstruction of the HV, a special detachment of *Sonderkommando LIn.3* was formed in Minden under the command of *Luftwaffe Leutnant* Reimar Horten.

The H Vc's engines were the same pair of 79 hp Hirth HM 60Rs from the unfortunate H Va. While this was just sufficient for a prototype, a quite different power was needed to combat the might of the Allied forces – with the United States just having

The cockpit of the first H IV was designed around its test pilot Heinz Scheidhauer, who was physically not very large. The later H IV models could accommodate larger pilots. Even Walter Horten (1.93 m) flew the H IV on one occasion. In order to relieve the pilot's back of the parachute weight, it was stored in a pocket under the cockpit hatch.

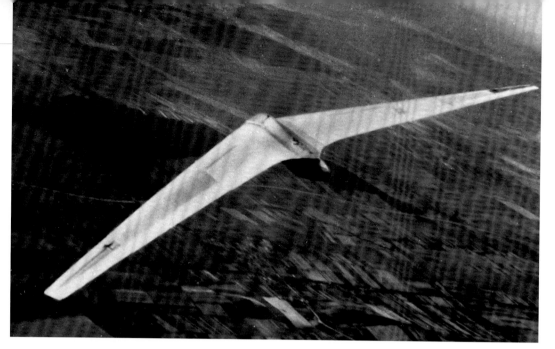

Left: The H IV in flight at the gliding school in Minden.

Below left and bottom: In the summer of 1941, when the German Wehrmacht pushed eastward into the Soviet Union, a Horten glider finally made some contribution to the German war effort. A H III with the fake registration D-15-1315 starred in the propaganda film 'Himmelhunde' produced on the orders of the Reichspropagandaministerium. This was filmed at the Nationalsozialistisches Fliegerkorps (NSFK) Reichssegelfliegerschule (gliding school) in Hornberg, 30 km west of Rottweil. The film was first aired in 1942 with the aim of winning young people for service in the Luftwaffe.

managed to obtain a technical description and performance graphs for the BMW 109-003 turbojet. This information quickly convinced the brothers that the turbojet was ideal for their all-wing aircraft.

The H Vc was completed and test-flown in Minden on 26 May 1942, sporting a *Luftwaffe*-style paint scheme and the registration PE+HO (denoting 'Peschke-Horten'). Later in that year, Walter Horten flew the machine to Göttingen, where *Sonderkommando LIn.3* was now quartered with its personnel expanded from nine to 30 men. In the autumn of 1942, Walter succeeded in obtaining a transfer to Göttingen, to take over command of the *Sonderkommando LIn.3*.[9] Due to Walter's efforts, the Horten team had been moved close to the Göttingen Aerodynamic Test Institute (AVA) with Reimar just avoiding a transfer to the *Fallschirmjäger* (paratroops). Now they had the opportunity to enlist military personnel from other units, choosing men with any amount of sailplane or aircraft-building experience. One of them was an 18 year-old soldier named Karl Nickel, who would remain with Reimar until the end of the war, performing aerodynamic and stress calculations and verifying flight performances for the majority of the Horten types.

In parallel to the H Vc, another powered Horten wing was being constructed during the winter of 1941/42. An H IIIb was equipped with a 48 hp Walter Mikron engine to become the H IIId motor-glider. Later dubbed '*die Butterfliege*'[10], the aircraft was test-flown on 29 June 1942, but due to teething problems the first powered flight did not take place before October of that year. The powerplant problems were finally solved with the installation of a more powerful 64-hp Walter Mikron engine.

The sole H IIId was to play a significant role in gaining the much needed credibility for the flying wing concept. The AVA director and leading German aerodynamicist, *Professor Dr.-Ing.* Ludwig Prandtl, believed, based on wind tunnel tests, that it

entered the war. The spectacular Walter rocket engine of the Me 163 was not suitable to power the long-range flying wing, as it would guzzle its propellant in minutes. Another solution – the turbojet engine, that was to comprise both great power and practicable fuel consumption – was already under development by the Heinkel, BMW and Junkers companies. Merely a month after the Me 163's record-breaking flight, Walter Horten

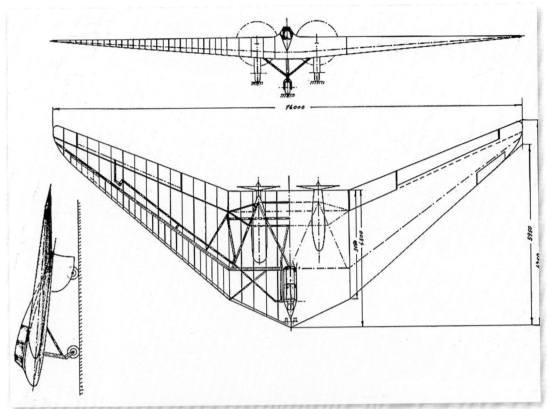

A three-view drawing of the H Vc.

As a Luftwaffe aircraft, the H Vc was repainted in a dull military livery of RLM 71 on its uppersurfaces and RLM 65 on the lower surfaces, with a Hakenkreuz applied to the outer sides of the undercarriage spats.

A pilot enters the cockpit of the H Vc.

The Horten H Vc.

The H Vc in flight.

was impossible to safely stall a tailless aircraft. In February 1943, a demonstration flight of the H IIId was arranged for Prandtl, *Professor Dr. Albert Betz* and others, in which Heinz Scheidhauer proved those fears groundless. Scheidhauer performed various manoeuvres with the motorglider – pulling the nose up until the airspeed was zero, then putting it down to regain speed and control response – showing no tendency to enter a spin. These manoeuvres were all flown at the dangerous height of no more than ten metres and were all safely executed without any loss of height. During the demonstration Reimar explained to Prandtl his ideas, techniques of wing twist and differentiated elevon deflection. This demonstration impressed Prandtl enough to revise his assumptions and to withdraw his warning to the industry against using swept-back wings because of the danger of stall spin. This fact is quite noteworthy since during this time Reimar Horten took classes with both professors at the University of Göttingen. He could often be seen riding on a bicycle in officer's uniform from the airfield to attend the lectures.

While the H Vc was being tested, its designers were already conceiving the next step to the all-wing fighter. In 1942 the *Luftwaffe* was looking for a suitable flying test-bed for the Schmitt-Argus pulsejet. In one of the tests, the acoustic pressure from the prototype engine destroyed a rudder of the Bf 110 test-bed. A thought was therefore given to adopting a tailless aircraft for this task, so the Hortens were asked about the suitability of the H Vc. Since preliminary calculations showed that this aircraft was rather light for handling the extra thrust from the pulsejet, the Hortens offered their earlier H VII twin-engine project. This flying wing had the same span but four times more power from two 236 hp Argus As10SC engines. The exhaust pipe of the pulse jet engine was to run between the two pushing two-blade constant-speed propellers. The propeller blades could be feathered in case of an engine failure and jettisoned for a safe bale out. The crew of two was accommodated in a tandem

The H IIId at Göttingen.

Professor Dr. Ludwig von Prandtl, centre, with the Horten brothers, observes the flight of the H IIId at Göttingen.

arrangement just ahead of the main spar of the centre section. The undercarriage comprised a twin leg nose gear retracting backwards and main gears retracting forwards with the wheels rotating through 90 degrees to lie flat below the wing surface. For directional control the usual drag spoilers were used initially, replaced after about 10 flights with a new type of rudder (tongue rudder), featuring wooden bars extending from the wingtips, sliding on ball bearings along the span. They did not perform very well so they were replaced again by the original drag spoilers.

Professor Dr. Albert Betz, who assisted Ludwig Prandtl in the development of efficient wing shape for sub- and supersonic speeds. Together with Prandtl, Betz witnessed a successful flight of the H IIId in February 1943.

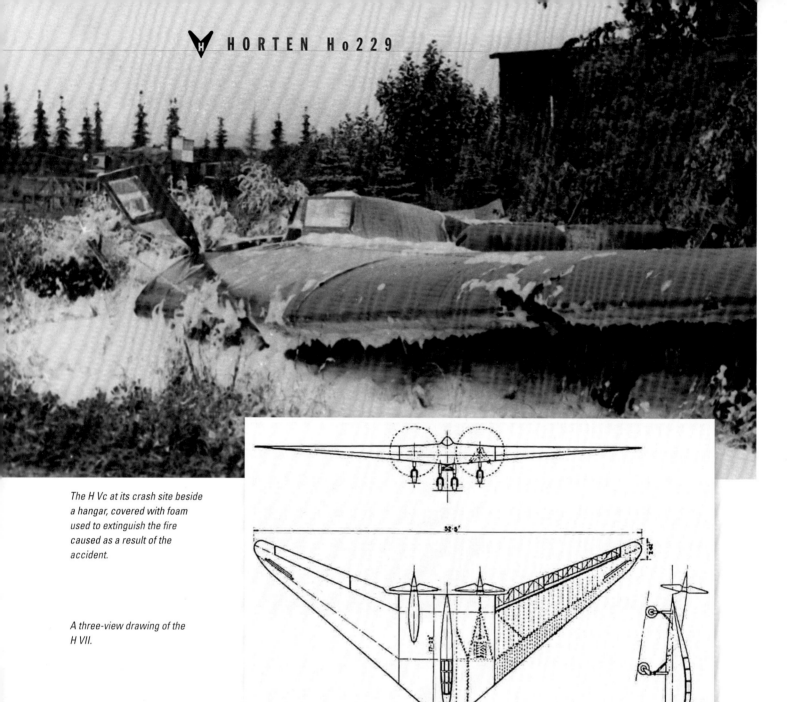

The H Vc at its crash site beside a hangar, covered with foam used to extinguish the fire caused as a result of the accident.

A three-view drawing of the H VII.

Assembly of the first prototype of the H VII at the Peschke works in Minden.

The new project was officially authorised under designation 8-254, and its development commenced at the *Sonderkommando LIn.3* in Göttingen, which was also to produce the wooden outer wings. Construction of the all-metal centre section, comprising a steel tubular framework with Dural skinning, and final assembly of the aircraft, was subcontracted to the Peschke plant in Minden.

The headquarters of the Horten team was housed in a converted *Reichsautobahnmeisterei* (*Autobahn* workshop) on the southern edge of Göttingen airfield about 100 m from the main *Autobahn* into the city. There was a hangar, a drawing office, machine and woodworking shops and other facilities placed at the Hortens' disposal. They had 'free' *Luftwaffe* personnel under their command, but no money. All materials and payments they needed they processed through an elaborate bureaucratic mechanism that Walter had perfected during their happy days under the

The twin-nose landing gear of the H VII bore 40 to 50 % of the total aircraft weight, which was 10-15 % heavier than usual.

Above left: Static-load testing of the outer wings of the H VII V1.

Here, the rear portions of the engine cowlings have been removed, showing the propeller extension shafts.

patronage of the now deceased Udet. Walter cultivated many contacts throughout the *Luftwaffe*, but perhaps his most important connection was made with Udet's former chief secretary, *Fräulein* von der Groeben. She processed the 'top secret' telegrams from *Sonderkommando LIn.3* with its requests for resources and sent them further along the RLM channels. The link worked so smoothly that nobody within the senior echelons of the RLM really scrutinized the Hortens' activity for a long time.

In May 1943 Walter married *Fräulein* von der Groeben; yet despite concerted efforts by the couple, all activities of the *Sonderkommando LIn.3* had been officially terminated by a RLM telegram in March 1943 following cancellation of the H VII project.

A little later, the H Vc programme also came to a sudden end. The aircraft was seriously damaged during take-off in the summer of 1943, during tests by *Flugkapitän Professor* Joseph Stüper of the AVA. Stüper started the H Vc from the middle of the airfield with the flaps erroneously set to the landing position. Consequently, the aircraft failed to gain altitude and crashed into the roof of a hangar, then dropped off the building.

Repair was postponed until after the war, but this never materialised. Neither did the plans to produce the H Vc-derived glider tug and the H Vd single-and two-seat (tail gunner) production versions.

Despite the moderate success of their early all-wing fighter prototypes, the idea was still only in the process of 'maturing' with the Horten brothers. A turbojet-powered version of the H VII was drawn up, but rejected in the spring of 1942, giving way to the new H IX, stressed for jet power from the start.

The H VII V1 at Göttingen.

Presentation of the H VII V1 to Luftwaffe officials. Note the extended starboard drag rudder.

Detailed view of the H VII's pusher propellers and the extension shafts cowlings.

The H VII V1 is seen taxiing at Göttingen.

The H VII V1 in flight.

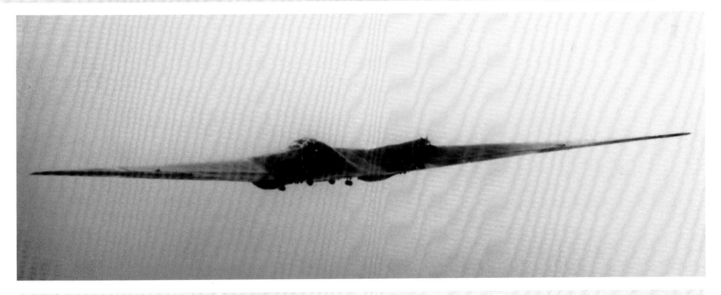

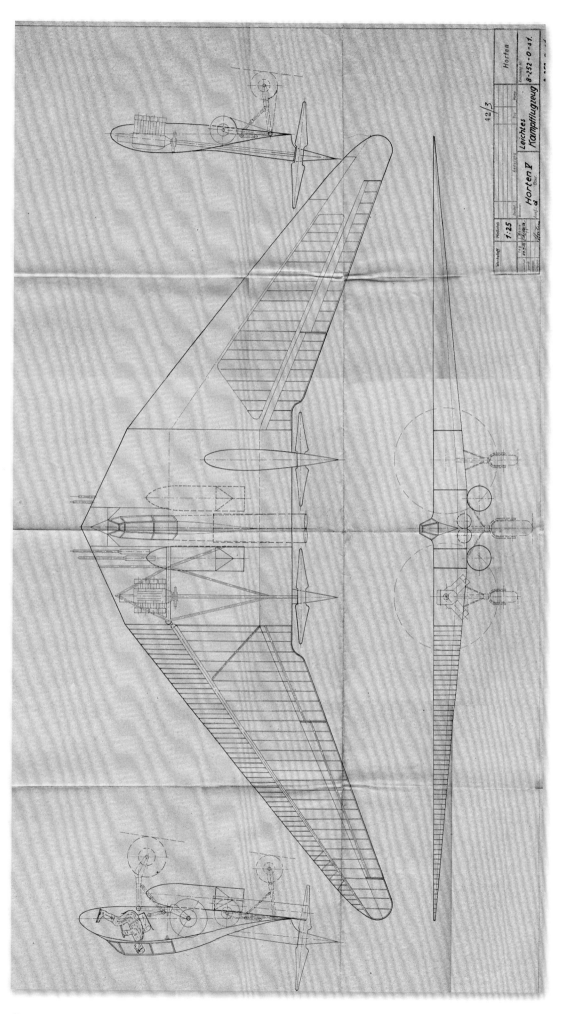

A drawing of the H V-based 'Leichtes Kampfflugzeug' dated 23 March 1942. Note the outline of what appears to be the two Argus Rohre pulsejets beneath the centreline of the aircraft.

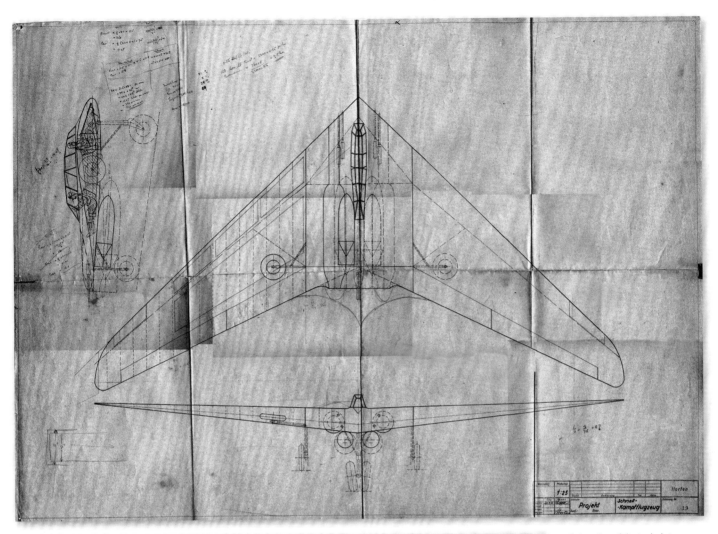

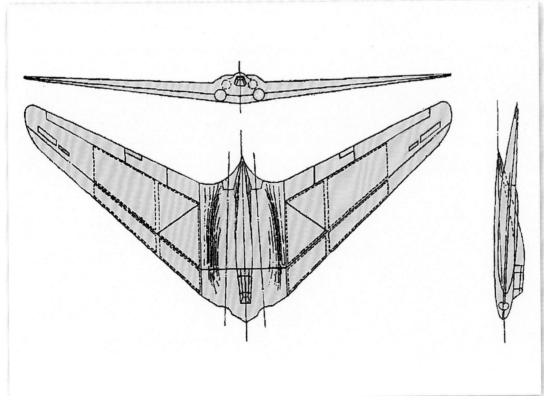

A drawing of the turbojet-powered version of the H VII Schnell-Kampfflugzeug, dated 26 March 1942, with the second crew member facing backwards to operate the defensive gun installation. Note the 'Horten-tail' pencilled to the original straight trailing edge, outward-retracting main undercarriage and the early type brake-rudders. The position of the engines and the bombs (drawn oversized) appears to be problematic in regard to obtaining a correct c/g. The signature on the drawing is that of Walter Horten.

The earliest general arrangement drawing of the H IX known to the writers. This sketch is different from the later design in having a shorter H IV-style 'bat-tail' and the H Vc-style segmented flat-panel canopy with its fairing extending all the way back to the tail tip.

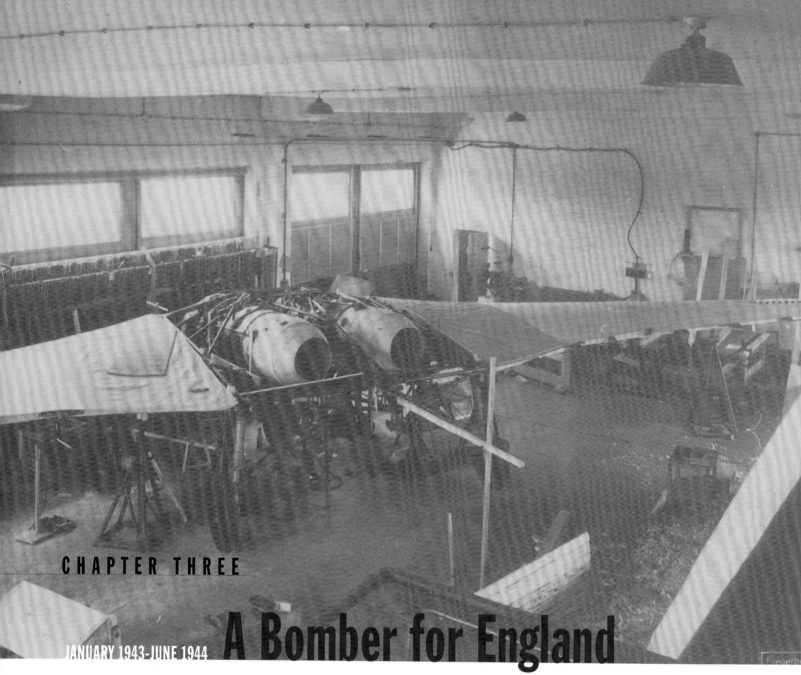

CHAPTER THREE

A Bomber for England

JANUARY 1943-JUNE 1944

Major Ulrich Diesing, a Ritterkreuzträger and a former Zerstörer pilot, who became Technical Officer to Reichsmarschall Göring. Diesing considered the Hortens' performance projections for the H IX unachievable. The Hortens subsequently blamed him for slow decision-making with regard to their proposals.

O NLY a few days before the German defeat at the battle for Stalingrad, another event had already marked a turning point in the course of the Second World War. On 27 January 1943, American bombers carried out their first attack on Germany from bases in England. Three days later RAF bombers attacked Hamburg in force at night, using the 8-centimetre H2S radar for the first time – a system which allowed precision bombing in zero visibility. The raids marked the beginning of a new Allied bombing offensive, which would continue almost uninterrupted until the war's end.

The German air defence, although formed around a highly elaborate system of fighter aircraft and Flak guided by ground and airborne radar, was wholly unable to deter the thousands of British and American bombers, and the growing Allied electronic warfare which further reduced its capabilities. The RAF continued to deliver powerful night attacks on German cities. On 1 March 1943, RAF bombers dropped 600 tons of bombs on Berlin, driving Hitler to order the resumption of the 'vengeance' attacks on London. The next night the *Luftwaffe* delivered 100 tons of

bombs to London, of which only a few fell within the city's boundaries. An infuriated *Führer* demanded from *Reichsmarschall* Hermann Göring "… an intensification of the air war against Britain", for which task a high-speed high-altitude bomber was to be fielded as soon as possible. The aircraft in question was planned to be the long-awaited Heinkel He 177, but this troubled machine was still far from entering operations.

A radical bomber that would allow the *Luftwaffe* to defy the Western Allies' numerical superiority was still to be invented. One week earlier, Göring had reluctantly approved the aircraft production plan for the coming year. This envisaged no new aircraft types. The *Luftwaffe* was operating no fewer than 16 different types of twin-engined warplanes, none of which could match the British Mosquito high-speed bomber. Such was Göring's admiration and envy for this beautiful *wooden* aeroplane, that he repeatedly demanded, against resistance, that the German aircraft industry copy it and match it in terms of performance. Thus in March 1943[11] Göring proclaimed in his stormy speech before the industry conference, that no more projects should be endorsed, unless they promised to carry a

The H IIIf in flight. Only a small canopy over the pilot's head protruded above the wing surface.

1,000 kg bombload 1,000 km into enemy territory at a speed of 1,000 km/h.

The bold '1000-1000-1000' requirement (1,000 kg x 1,000 km x 1,000 km/h) was not the *Reichsmarschall's* personal proposal. In fact, it echoed the demands of the RLM's Technical Department as summarised in the 20 October 1942 *'Guidelines for Aircraft Development'*. The report asked, amongst other things, for the creation of a high-speed medium bomber with a one-ton payload, possessing a 'penetration depth' of 1,046 km and a top speed of 700 km/h. The penetration depth was defined as one third of the quite impressive total range, while the speed was to be later increased to the speed of sound (1,000-plus km/h at operational altitudes).[12] In the style of the Mosquito, the modest bombload was to be delivered with pinpoint accuracy to key targets – primarily British airfields, while the aircraft's immunity from interception was to shatter the enemy's morale and – supposedly – its will to fight.

Years later both of the Horten brothers would claim that it was Walter who brought the '1000-1000-1000' concept to Göring's attention. Acting through the *Reichsmarschall's* Technical Officer, *Major* Ulrich Diesing, the Hortens' intention was to promote their H IX fighter concept as one capable of fulfilling the new bomber requirements. Despite the obvious fact that the desired performance figures by far exceeded the state-of-the-art of the time, the Hortens believed that the efficiency of the all-wing configuration would come close to the requirements. Reimar prepared a 20 page H IX proposal for Göring, but Diesing chose to circulate the paper first throughout the RLM departments for review. He deemed the goal unachievable for a company whose speed record to date was only 280 km/h, whereas even reputable firms did not dare to submit their proposals.[13]

Despite the disbanding of the Horten team, the brothers' work continued throughout the spring and summer of 1943. The concept of the proposed

Pilot accommodation in the cockpit of the H IIIf.

Nurflügel jet was outlined by the Hortens in their report presented on 14 April 1943 in Berlin before the *Lilienthal Gesellschaft* conference, during which a heated debate for and against the flying wing took place. Kurt Tank, Hans Multhopp and Alexander Lippisch presented pro and counter arguments, while several professors from Darmstadt, Braunschweig and Berlin-Adlershof immediately dismissed the concept offhand. In their report the Hortens cited a recently published book titled *'Aerodynamics of the flying model'* by their teacher F.W.Schmitz, but no mention of the 'bell-shaped lift distribution' theory was documented in the conference's papers.

Nevertheless, no less than half a year had been lost for the H IX project since March 1943, for which the Hortens later alternatively blamed either Diesing's slow decision-making, or their own numerous works-in-progress. In parallel to the H IX and H Vc programmes, the H IV glider was further pursued under the official designation 8-251 (Ho 251), with three more examples, modified to

The LA-AC and LA-AD (right) were the last H IVa gliders built in Göttingen in mid-summer 1943.

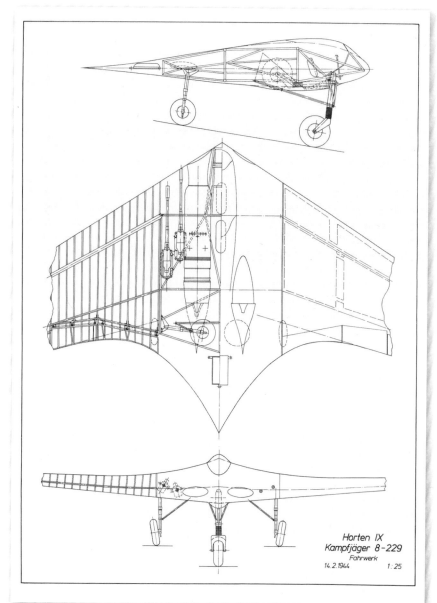

Horten IX
Kampfjäger 8-229
Fahrwerk
14.2.1944   1:25

The original draft layout of the BMW 109-003 powered H IX, dated 14 February 1944. Note the heavy armament of four long-barrel 30 mm MK 103 cannon with very little room left for ammunition. Landing gear components from the He 177 and Bf 109 were utilised for the nose and main legs respectively.

accommodate larger pilots, constructed in 1943. These were first flown at Göttingen on 11 February, 28 April and 20 June 1943 respectively. To ease the transition of pilots to the high-performance H IV, an H IIIb was modified into the H IIIf with a prone pilot position. In less than a year since mid-summer 1943, this glider had accumulated 100 flying hours at the Klippeneck glider school at the Schwäbische Alb.

At last, on 28 September 1943 the Horten brothers were summoned to Göring's Karinhall residence to present their '1000-1000-1000' proposal. What they showed to the *Reichsmarschall* was certainly one of the most unusual aircraft ever conceived…

Very little more than a pure wing constituted the shape of the Horten IX. There was neither a fuselage nor an empennage, and only the pilot's canopy and the exhaust ducts of the jet engines protruded above the upper surface of the swept-back wing. The engines were installed inside the centre section of the wing, slightly inclined nose-down with the air intakes positioned below the leading edge, while the exhausts were positioned half-buried into the wing.

Structurally the H IX was similar to most of the other Horten designs, comprising a steel tubular framework centre section with plywood covering and all-wooden outer wing panels. The plywood skin aft of the jet exhausts was protected by sheet steel plates installed with a clearance of 10 mm for cooling. The sheet steel was also used for engine cowlings and firewalls, air intakes, undercarriage doors and various hatches. Utilisation of 'non-strategic' materials such as wood and steel was considered favourable under conditions of increasing war-time shortages. Moreover, small dispersed workshops could be used for the manufacture of wooden parts using unskilled forced labour – another advantage for an industry whose factories were being bombed out and workers taken to the Front. It was also thought that the wooden wing would be less vulnerable to combat damage.

Most of the wing's control linkage and cables went inside the main spar, with 3,000 litres (around 2,500 kg)[14] of fuel required for achieving the

Horten IX Aerodynamic Layout and Control

A relatively conservative approach had been taken to the aerodynamic layout of the H IX, based heavily on available experience. The wing sweep was moderate at 32 degrees; the wingspan measured 16 metres, equalling the span of the H IX's predecessors H Vb/c and H VII, and the overall length was 6.5 metres. The trailing edge was curved to form a pointed bat-tail, similar to the H IV, but more pronounced, since the original 'T-4' parabola line was given a sharp bend backwards in a further attempt to overcome the persistent 'Mitten-Effekt'.

The wing section at the root was a Horten-designed reflexed camber-line type with a maximum camber of 2 %, transitioning into a symmetrical airfoil at the tips, with all sections in between being a straight-line interpolation. Maximum thickness was 15 % at 30 % of the chord at the centreline, 13 % at 30 % of the chord at the junction of the centre section with the outer wing panels, and 8 % at the wingtips. The wing had been designed with a maximum geometrical twist of -1 degrees at the wing tips. This, combined with an aerodynamic twist (the angle between the chord line and the zero-lift line of the airfoil) of -0.687 degrees, gave a total washout of -1.687 degrees. The wing twist was considerably less than that of the previous Horten aircraft, having been determined with the consideration of the critical Mach number of the local airflow at the underside of the wingtip section at maximum speed. This effectively precluded the adoption of Reimar's BSLD to the H IX. The aerodynamic layout of the H IX (as well as those of the H V and the H VII) provided for a minimal acceptable longitudinal static margin. Two-stage elevons and single-stage flaps occupied all of the outer wings' trailing edge. The outer elevons were of the Frise-type with 25 % compensation, the inner acting also as flaps (flaperons). The flaperons were compensated by kinematical superimposition to the outer elevons. The flaperons lowered 27 degrees (10 degrees for take-off), the inner flaps 30 degrees to -35 degrees. Longitudinal control was by differentiated deflections of the flaperons in +30 degrees to -5 degrees range and the elevons in +5 degrees to -30 degrees range, lateral control by deflections in +20 degrees to -2 degrees and +2 degrees to -20 degrees ranges respectively. For an effective directional control throughout the full speed range, two-stage drag rudders (spoilers) were envisaged at the upper and lower surfaces of the wingtips. A movement of the rudder pedals first opened the small outboard section, giving sufficient control at high speed; further movement opened also the bigger inboard section. The control input from the rudder pedals was transmitted via a cam plate, with the drag force of the airflow acting on the opening rudder being partly offset by a spring-loaded compensating device. This mechanism provided for a near-linear relationship between the pedal and rudder movements and a low operating force of 1 kg for full rudder, with a very slight variation in speed. For augmenting the control input forces from the pilot's control column during a high speed flight, a telescoping upper part was fitted to the stick that could extend some 5 centimetres (a similar device was also tested on the Messerschmitt Me 262 V10). Beneath the aft part of the centre section a spoiler was envisaged for glide-path control and for use as an airbrake, providing up to 0.33g of deceleration at maximum speed. Located further aft was a brake parachute compartment; the brake chute and the spoiler were intended to prevent the touchdown-delaying 'floating' during landing.

specified range to fill all remaining wing volume, using no separate tanks. The fuel-proof glue, necessary for sealing the inside of the 'wet-wing', had been developed by *Dr.* Pinton at Dynamit AG. This glue would also be used for the assembly of the wing and bonding the wooden structures with plastic and metal parts such as the H IX's wingtip metal panels. Since this glue was not yet available, eight separate metal tanks were envisaged as an intermediate solution, two ahead and two behind the main spars of both outer wings. Total fuel capacity of the tanks was only 2,400 litre / 2,000 kg, providing for a combat radius of 800 km (range of 1,880 km at 630 km/h, or 3,150 km with two 1,250 litre underslung tanks). In place of the jettisonable tanks two 1,000 kg bombs could be taken; the maximum speed was estimated to be 950-960 km/h, the calculated ceiling was 16,000 metres – although existing engines could not operate above 12,000 metres.

Although the Hortens' proposal fell just short of the '1000-1000-1000' specifications, it was far superior in terms of performance to anything the *Luftwaffe* had in its inventory. The *Reichsmarschall* was unquestionably impressed and approved the project immediately. Udet's successor *Generalfeldmarschall* Erhard Milch, present at the

meeting together with Major Diesing, was given the order to grant the Hortens a formal contract worth 500,000 *Reichsmarks*. This was soon signed with a newly established company in Bonn called Horten Flugzeugbau GmbH, which was contracted to design and construct three H IX prototypes. The H IX V1 was to be flown as a glider by 1 March 1944, while the jet-powered second prototype was ordered to be ready three months later. For the actual work, the Horten group – renamed *'Luftwaffen-Kommando IX'* – (Lw.Kdo IX) - was reactivated at the original Göttingen location under the command of *Hauptmann* Walter Horten with *Oberleutnant* Reimar Horten acting as deputy; their workforce soon grew to 200 men.

After the start of the project in the autumn of 1943, the Messerschmitt Company tried to take over the Horten group. This attempt was apparently not supported by the RLM because of Milch's long-lasting hostile relationship with Willy Messerschmitt. No less, if slightly veiled, was the *Generalfeldmarschall's* opposition to Göring. Although Milch evidently had no choice but to approve the Horten IX, which after all was based on his own requirements, only a month after signing the contract he pushed the project to a far corner of his desk. During a conference on aircraft

The Generalluftzeugmeister, Generalfeldmarschall Erhard Milch, placed manufacturing priority on the production of urgently needed fighters, tactical bombers and transports to service the escalating demands of Germany's multi-front war. Only a month after signing a contract for three H IX prototypes however, he pushed the project to a far corner of his desk, objecting to its priority status. Milch favoured instead the Arado Ar 234 jet and Dornier Do 335.

Horten IX Wing Design

Accommodation of the tanks across the wing ribs meant these were to be made hollow (the ribs located between the tanks were strengthened by removable internal struts to allow installation/removal of the tanks). At first, the wing was designed with an overall skinning of 8 mm, eight layer plywood. This construction proved sufficient for the H IX V1 glider, but after calculations were made it was discovered that this wing would not be stiff enough to withstand the forces at the anticipated high speeds of the later models. The required stiffness of the wing was therefore to be provided by doubling the skin thickness which would have resulted in a wing nose with a very thick skin of 16 mm. Birch plywood with a thickness of 16 mm proved too difficult to work with and therefore it was decided to use two sheets of 8 mm plywood with a sawdust core for bonding in between. This core would also be used to fill any irregularities.[15] The result was an unusually thick 17 mm wing nose skin while the rest of the wing was still covered by 8 mm plywood. (For comparison, the H VII's wing had a 2.5 mm plywood skin). Although adding considerably to the airframe weight, such a thick skin allowed the wing to withstand up to 12.6g of normal acceleration, which provided a safe load of 7g with a safety factor of 1.8.

Despite this impressive figure, it is not correct to assume the H IX could have made a 'super-agile' fighter. As a result of a request from the Jagdwaffe, the aircraft was to be armed with four 30 mm cannon, but its extremely low thrust-to-weight ratio and the slow throttle response of the existing jet engines would render the H IX not suitable for dog-fighting. Nevertheless, its airframe had been stressed to enable a complete aileron roll in four seconds at 900 km/h at 2,500 metres. Another design criterion was the ability to withstand the loads from gusts up to 10 m/sec in a dive at 1,100 km/h, with a safety factor of 1.2. The wing stiffness was sufficient to prevent aileron reversal at speeds up to 1,320 km/h. All these criteria were obviously based on an optimistic forecast for the maximum speed.

development on 29 October 1943, Milch objected to placing the order for three Horten IX prototypes into the highest priority (DE) rating. He believed this could only be done at the cost of other high priority projects such as the Arado Ar 234 jet bomber/reconnaissance aircraft, and his personal favourite, the Dornier Do 335 tandem-propeller fighter-bomber. In his opinion the H IX would not become operational before 1947 because, as Inspector-General, Deputy Commander-in-Chief of the *Luftwaffe* and Chief of the Technical Department of the RLM, he knew only too well that a new aircraft took an average of four years to get from the drawing board to an operational unit. The RLM Chief of Procurement and Supply (GL/C) was therefore given the order to re-evaluate the list of top-priority projects.

In contrast to this, a contract to the same specification was given to Alexander Lippisch to develop his earlier P.11 project of late 1942. By this time Lippisch took over the position of director of the Aeronautical Research Institute (*Luftfahrtforschung Wien*, LFW) in Vienna, where he had moved with most of his group after leaving Messerschmitt in April 1943.

With a low priority assigned to the project, the Hortens were left to recycle the many necessary parts from scrapped aircraft at the Göttingen test facility. In this way, the He 177 tail wheel assembly complete with retraction mechanism, became the nose-landing gear on the first two H IX prototypes. The massive nose-wheel bore up to 40-50% of the aircraft's weight (originally planned was an H VII-type twin nose gear). The main landing gear of both the H IX V1 and the V2 consisted of two modified Bf 109G units, and parts from a damaged Me 210 were also utilised. Electric fuel pumps and other components came from a captured B-24 Liberator.

At the same time when the personnel of 'Kommando IX' at Göttingen worked day and night to meet the deadline set for the first flight of the H IX V1, the Horten brothers embarked on a yet another ambitious project. The goal of their new H X was to explore the benefit of the all-wing's sweep-back that had been found by Busemann to delay the transonic shock stall. While the H IX's aerodynamic design was based heavily on that of its slow-speed predecessors in order to reduce the developmental risk, a higher sweep-back was to be considered for achieving transonic speeds. Following their customary routine, the Hortens started with flying models, followed by the construction of an experimental glider, named the H XIIIa (instead of the H Xa) for security reasons. Upon exploration of the low-speed handling of the highly-swept glider, a prop-powered version with an Argus As 10C pusher engine was to be tested prior to the jet-powered transonic prototype.

This work was kept secret, as the brothers rightfully did not expect the RLM to approve such a bold idea. The whole project was hidden in a converted *Autobahn* workshop in Bad Hersfeld 70 km south of Göttingen.

Before the H XIIIa could be taken into the air, work on the H XI aerobatic sailplane was started in Bad Hersfeld but was never finished. Next in the series, the H XII was a commercial two-seater designed around a 90 hp DKW six-cylinder car engine used as an auxiliary powerplant in the He 177. Another sporting aircraft, the H IIIe motor-glider, was built by the Hortens as a private project and made its first flight on 25 January 1944. It was powered by a 29.5 hp Volkswagen engine taken directly from a car. The engine could be shut down in-flight with the propeller blades automatically folding to lessen the drag, and could then easily be started again, using the standard battery and starter; even the exhaust muffler was retained. In such a

Horten craftsmen fit together the wooden elements of the centre section covering of the H IX V1.

way, the glider could be flown for hours, soaring once from Göppingen to Frankfurt. Walter later regarded this beautiful touring airplane, along with the H VII, to be the best all-round Horten design.

At the same time, the long-planned H VI (8-253) high-performance sailplane was being completed in a converted dance hall at Aegidienberg near Bonn. The purpose of this aircraft, of which the construction cost some 8,000 man-hours, was claimed to be the investigation of the *'Mitten-Effekt'* on its H IX-style pointed tail. The very high aspect ratio of 32.4 was allegedly necessary to move the elevons farther outside the test area. In fact, this model had been conceived as early as 1941 for record-breaking purposes, while the enlarged 'bat-tail' was first tried on the H IX itself.

The H IX V1 was ready by 1 March 1944 – on schedule as set by the contract. Bad weather prevented the first flight on that day, so the aircraft was photographed with the date signed on a placard posted in front of it, and the photograph was sent to Göring.[16] According to the other version of events, on 1 March 1944 Heinz Scheidhauer took the H IX V1 into the air. Towed by a small Heinkel He 45 biplane, the heavy glider performed two short hops along Göttingen airfield.[17] Walter asked the RLM about the availability of a more powerful Heinkel He 111, and the Ministry made this tow-plane and its pilot available.

The Hortens happened to know the pilot, *Leutnant* Erwin Ziller, from the Wasserkuppe gliding competitions, while Scheidhauer knew him even better. In May 1940 both Ziller and Scheidhauer fought shoulder-to-shoulder in the famed Eben-Emael operation as pilots of DFS 230 assault gliders. Their mounts, coded '6' and '7'

respectively, landed at the northern flank of the fort, with Scheidhauer being injured in the process. Ziller later served as a glider instructor at Parchim, before becoming a factory test pilot at Focke-Wulf.

The 'actual' maiden flight of the H IX V1 was performed by Scheidhauer on 5 March 1944. The towing He 111 blew a large cloud of snow from the airstrip, blinding the pilot of the H IX V1 behind it, but Scheidhauer soon managed to get the glider above the cloud and the tow proceeded uneventfully. Following release at 3,600 metres, the H IX V1 glided back to Göttingen. Scheidhauer had to overfly a hangar in a steep approach, so that he was still quite high at the beginning of the runway. Due to the ground effect the aircraft 'floated' until touchdown in the middle of the airfield. The brake chute was released but was too small and the wheel-brakes did not help much because of the slippery snow on the ground. To avoid the risk of collision with a hangar ahead, Scheidhauer retracted the front wheel and stopped the aircraft on its nose long before the building.

An early version of the wing of the H IX V1. The control rods were connected to the elevon's spar through a skew hinge, allowing concealment of the entire linkage within the wing.

At the end of February 1944, the H IX V1 was rolled out of the garage where it had been assembled, and towed by truck to the main hangar at Göttingen, where the outer wings were attached.

Heinz Scheidhauer lies on the port wing of the H IX V1.

The Heinkel He 111 tow plane, with engines running, prepares to take the H IX V1 aloft.

Below: A groundcrew member signals to the He 111 that the H IX V1 is ready to start.

The H IX V1 with its nose buried in the snow-covered airstrip some 100 m before the hangar on 5 March 1944. Heinz Scheidhauer was forced to retract the nose wheel to avoid a collision on the ground during his landing run after his first test flight.

Ground crew use an inflatable bag to raise the H IX V1, so that the nose wheel can be extended.

After two further flights on 23 March 1944, tests continued from the long concrete runway of Oranienburg airfield near Berlin. There, on 5 April 1944, the nosewheel failed after developing a shimmy during the landing run. Following this accident the nosewheel was modified with torque scissors.[18] The V1 was flown again by Scheidhauer on 20 April 1944, before being brought back to Göttingen. In early April the RLM sent a team from the *Deutsche Versuchsanstalt fur Luftfahrt* (DVL) at Berlin-Adlershof to instrument the V1 for stability and controllability tests aimed at determining the H IX's suitability as a gun platform. One of the instruments used was a four metre-long swivelling incidence-measuring pole that was broken in the final test flight when the pilot forgot to retract it before landing.

The 10-page test report by the DVL that followed on 7 July 1944[19] pointed to directional oscillation of an abnormally long eight-second period, which damped out slower than usual, in five cycles at 250 km/h. According to the report, at low speeds the aircraft developed 'Dutch-roll' type lateral/-directional oscillation.

Control harmonisation is an issue with the all-wing configuration due to its high ratio of lateral inertia to longitudinal inertia. This ratio depends on the actual design geometry, decreasing with higher sweep angles and increasing with higher aspect ratio. It topped therefore to 30:1 on the extreme H VI, which had been first flown on 24 May 1944

On 5 April 1944 the H IX V1 continued with trials on the concrete runway at Fliegerhorst Oranienburg. There the nose wheel collapsed again after developing a shimmy during the landing run.

by Heinz Scheidhauer. Although this peculiarity could be acceptable for a soaring glider, with a low longitudinal inertia even favourable when trying to turn tightly at low speed to stay in thermals, the extra-high aspect-ratio Horten was never to fulfil its promise. Neither was it to bring any benefit to the H IX programme. During the half-hour maiden flight of the H VI V1 (W.Nr.33, LA-AK), its excessively flexible wings developed a dangerous flutter commencing at about 110-120 km/h and this characteristic denied the glider any future success.

For a warplane like the H IX, its lateral to longitudinal inertia ratio of 5:1 could have rendered control harmonisation – and hence accurate aiming – difficult. On the other hand, there was a widely discussed view within the DVL that the period of directional oscillation on a high-speed fighter should be at least four seconds long to enable the pilot to stabilise the aircraft for accurate gunnery. Not surprisingly, Reimar adhered to this theory in his arguments with the RLM over the frequency and duration of the directional oscillations on the H IX. As an expedient measure for steadying the aircraft during aiming, both drag-rudders could be opened simultaneously by pressing both rudder pedals at once.

Regardless of the DVL measurements, Scheidhauer reported very good directional stability of the H IX V1. Although it was equipped with large fin-like spats covering the main undercarriage legs, these did not significantly augment the directional

stability because of the small momentum in relation to the c/g, so an acceptable directional stability could be also expected for the powered versions of the aircraft which omitted the spats.[20]

By the time of the V1's first flight, the second prototype of the H IX was in the assembly stage, awaiting its engines. Before the disbanding of *Sonderkommando* LIn.3 in March 1943, Walter had been able to order two 109-003 turbojets from BMW's Berlin-Spandau works. Since there were still no airworthy BMW 003s available, the Bavarian motor company initially delivered to the Hortens two empty engine shells to be used as development mock-ups. Upon delivery of an operational engine, it was planned to test it beneath the H VII flying test-bed. Meanwhile, in October 1943 BMW-Spandau issued a description of the installation of the pre-series BMW 003A-0 engines in the Horten aircraft. The engines were to be delivered in standard form but had to be modified to fit inside the wing.

Construction of the H IX prototype with the BMW 003 casings installed was under way, when *Dr.* Hermann Oesterich, BMW's director of turbojet development, informed the Hortens that availability of the 109-003 was delayed to an undefined date. Fortunately, there was another turbojet of similar performance, which was nearing production stage at the Junkers Motorenbau (Jumo) in Dessau.

Details of this alternative powerplant became first known to the Hortens in January 1942 when Walter brought drawings of the Jumo 109-004 to Reimar in Minden. Various configurations had been considered for the H IX's propulsion system, including a mixture of two Argus pulsejets with a Jumo 004 mounted underneath. In March 1943 Walter had obtained the performance curves and installation drawings for this turbojet. He had also had access to the top-secret Jumo 004-powered Me 262 fighter[21] and data pertaining to it. The Jumo was approximately 100 kg heavier than the BMW 003, but it gave 100 kg more thrust.

Therefore, Walter inquired of Junkers' chief of turbojet development, *Dr.* Anselm Franz, about the possible availability of the 109-004. He was

The H IX V1 approaches the airfield with its landing gear down.

The H IX V1 is towed back to its hangar after one of the test flights.

promised the delivery of two units worth 50,000 *Reichsmarks* each, but not before March 1944. Meanwhile, one run-out 109-004 prototype was delivered to the Hortens to be used as a mock-up. This engine was larger than the BMW 003, although the forward (compressor) section that was to fit inside the main spar, had roughly the same diameter of 60 centimetres. The tubular framework of the H IX V2's centre section was modified to accommodate the run-out 109-004, as was its air intake. The original design employed an elegant oval opening on the underside of the leading edge, the airflow fed to the engine through a slightly curved duct. Whether this curvature would not entail air disturbances at the engine's inlet, could not be guaranteed though, so instead the air intake was cut straight through the leading edge.

The two airworthy Jumo 004 B-1 turbojets were delivered to the Hortens a few weeks late, in mid-April 1944. The irony was that it was the first time the brothers were able to see how the complete engine should look. The Horten *Kommandos'* special position as a *Luftwaffe* unit outside the direct control of the RLM gave them a bad service this time, leaving them without a timely update on the latest version of the engine. They were astonished to discover accessories mounted to the compressor casing, which increased its height to 0.8 m. Now there was simply not enough space for the casing and accessories to pass between the spar-booms already built to accommodate an engine with a 0.6 m diameter.

The accessories could be dismantled before mounting/dismounting the engine, and could be re-fitted later – this troublesome and time-consuming procedure was actually undertaken on the H IX. However, there remained temperature and maintenance concerns about the reduced clearance between the engine and the structure. Even worse, the accessory drive mounted at the front top of the compressor casing would protrude from the surface of the wing nose.

A straightforward solution to the problem appeared to be to simply rotate the engine ninety degrees about its longitudinal axis, so that the protruding parts would fit within the existing airframe structure. *Dr.* Franz of Jumo

The H IX V1 at Göttingen: note the torque scissors added to the nose-landing gear. The wing is different from that used during early test fights. The inner elevon sections (flaperons) are equipped with what appears to be a servo tab; the outer elevons have trim tabs added.

Although the uppersurface of the H IX V1 looks rather light in this picture, the colour is in fact dark green (most probably RLM 71). The underside was painted light blue (RLM 65). Over the standard finish all surfaces were coated with glossy shellac. A wing-walk area was bordered by a continuous stripe. A sign at the trailing edge reads, possibly, 'Hier betreten'. To the right of the sign is the stencilled manufacturer's table.

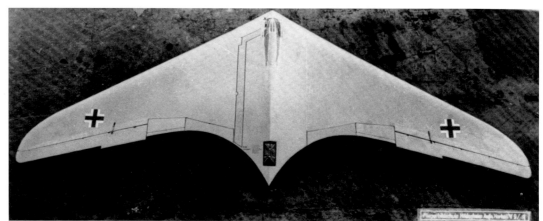

The H IX V1 cockpit. The undercarriage well opening below the pilot's seat is sealed with canvas.

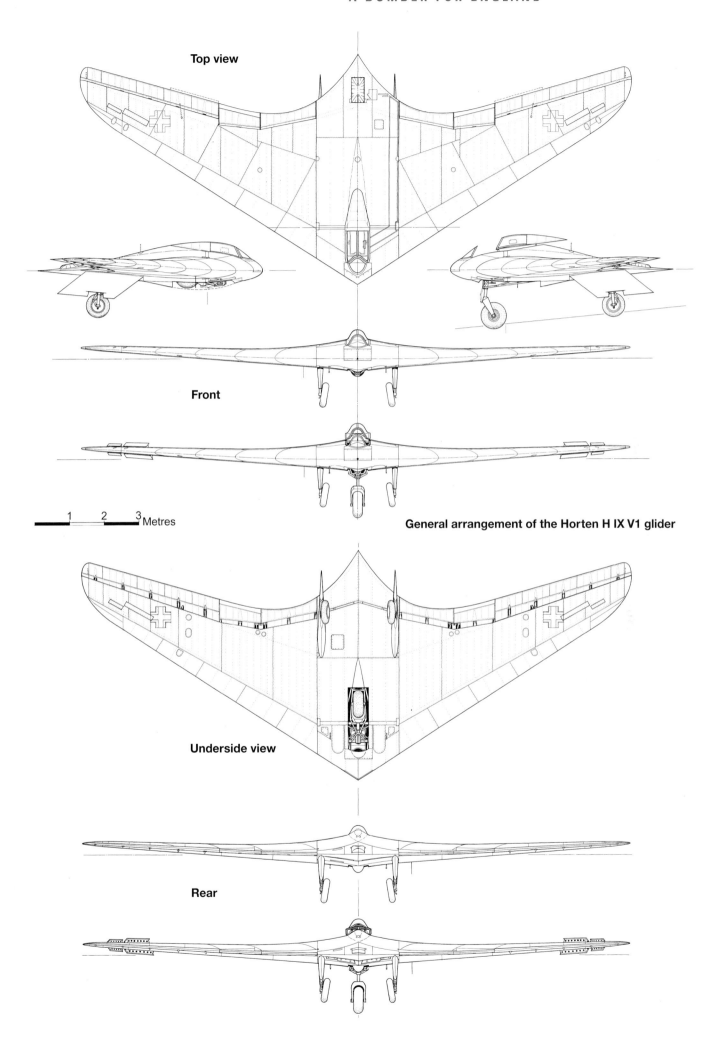

Top view

Front

Underside view

Rear

1 2 3 Metres

General arrangement of the Horten H IX V1 glider

Top view

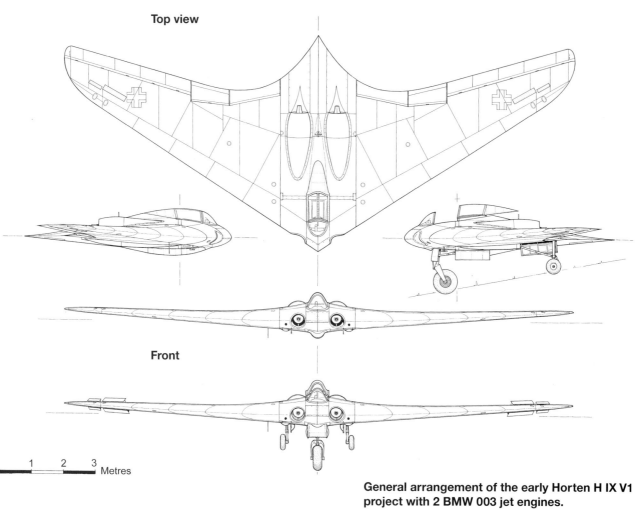

Front

1 2 3
Metres

General arrangement of the early Horten H IX V1
project with 2 BMW 003 jet engines.

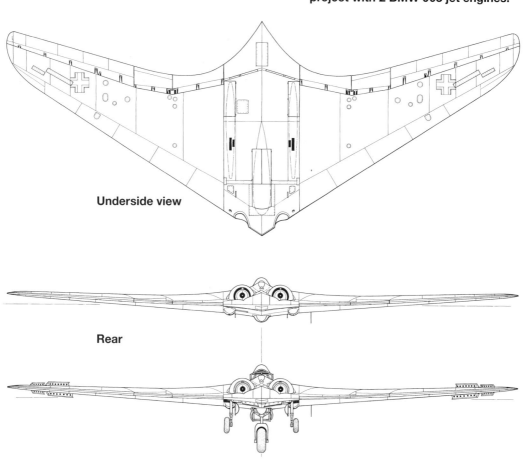

Underside view

Rear

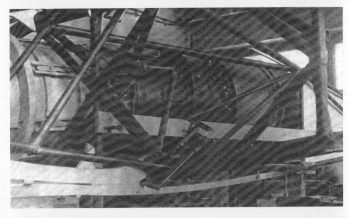

Construction of the original H IX V2 centre section with the prototype BMW 003 engine shell installed. Note the 'bottle-neck' air ducts, and the temporary central nose rib that evidently served only to help form the nose profile. This illustrates the Hortens' approach to combine the prototype and mock-up stages of development.

The BMW 003 engine.

The Jumo 004 engine.

Dr. Anselm Franz, chief of turbojet development at Junkers, agreed to the Hortens' design amendments to accommodate two Jumo 004 B-1 turbojets within the H IX.

the converted furniture factory of Ortlepp in Friedrichroda. As it happened, this dispersal facility in the small Thuringian town near the city of Gotha was soon to become a home for the Horten IX.

To prevent deterioration of the H IX's projected performance, it was decided to retain as much of the original design as possible. The outer wing panels remained the same, but their root profile thickness grew from 13% to 13.8%, further increasing along the centre section to 15.3% at the aircraft's centreline. As a compromise solution, the engines were rotated 15 degrees outwards to fit into the centre section. The RLM gave permission to Reimar to remove the annular tank for starting fuel and the oil tank/cooler in front of the engine, since these did not fit inside the wing nose. An alternative oil tank obviously had to be provided elsewhere, outside the original position where the cooling would have been most effective.

The centre section had been widened, as compared to the H IX V1, from 2.4 to 3.2 metres by adding a new centreline rib '00' 0.4 metres outside the original rib '0'. The overall length of the aircraft increased proportionally from 6.5 to 7.47 metres. Reimar Horten later attributed this modification to the changes in the engine configuration. In fact, the early BMW 003-powered H IX already had the enlarged centre section. The reason for changing the original V1 geometry was probably to provide adequate room for the cannon installation.

The increased wingspan led to a marginally greater geometrical twist of 1.05 degrees. The thicker wing sections reduced the critical Mach number to 0.75, corresponding to 920 km/h at sea level and 797 km/h at 12,000 metres. One positive outcome of the changes was a forward shift in the centre of gravity that was thought to remove the need for ballast. In fact, the unarmed V2 did need 232 kg of lead ballast for an appropriate c/g location, which reduced the fuel storage to 2,000 l / 1,700 kg.

Thus, the geometry and structure of the centre section changed at least four times during the construction of the H IX V2 – in a style typical for the Hortens which seemed more like building a mock-up. Although the basic aerodynamic design and general arrangement were carefully worked out by Reimar, detail work was usually relegated to workshop level, with parts first tried out on the actual aircraft before being drawn on paper. This practice in fact reflected the nature of an integrated all-wing design, whereby any significant changes in its particular components often led to the revision of the entire layout.

approved this installation but, for unknown reasons, the RLM did not allow the Hortens to proceed.

Obviously, applying any kind of fairing was out of the question for Reimar, so the wing had to be made thicker to accommodate the larger engines. In the case of a simple scaling up the span would increase from 16 to 21.3 metres, and the wing area from 42 to 75 m². This would make an aircraft as large as a conventional twin-engine bomber, with no hope of achieving the required speed.

In an interesting parallel, this was also the size of another all-wing twin Jumo 004-powered aircraft project, which had been under development since late 1943 at Gothaer Waggonfabrik (GWF) under the leadership of *Dr. Ing.* Hünerjäger and *Dr. Ing.* Rudolf Göthert. The P-53Z heavy *Zerstörer* and *Nachtjäger* had a wingspan of 22.4 metres, a length of 14.25 metres and a height of 5.54 metres and was aimed at replacing the licence-built Bf 110 at the GWF assembly lines. This factory, best known by the name of its home town, 'Gotha', contributed to almost one-third of Germany's twin-engine aircraft production before being heavily damaged during a raid on 24 February 1944 by US Eighth Air Force Liberator bombers.

While the Hortens were looking for a solution to squeeze the turbojets into the H IX, Gotha decided in mid-April 1944 to commence with the construction of the cumbersome P-53Z mock-up at

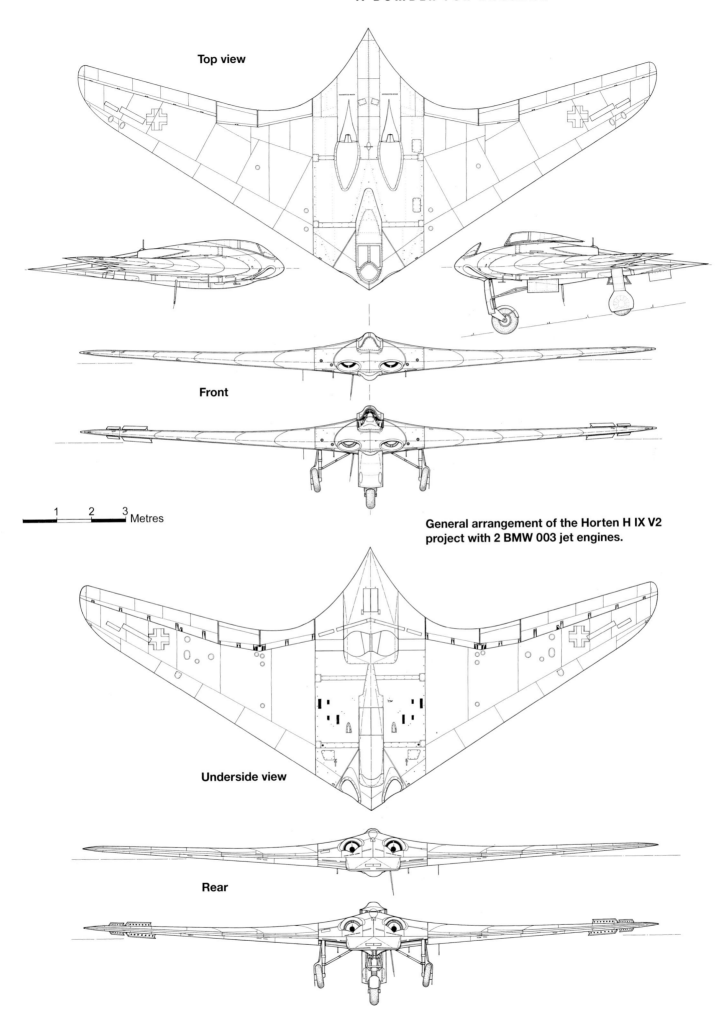

Top view

Front

Underside view

Rear

1 2 3 Metres

General arrangement of the Horten H IX V2 project with 2 BMW 003 jet engines.

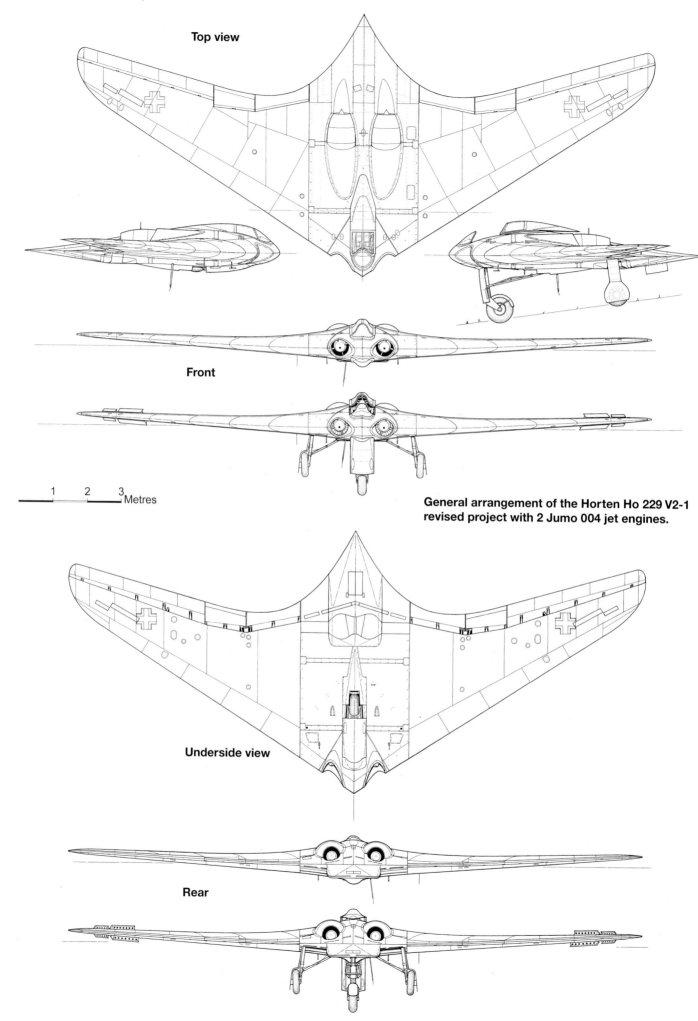

Top view

Front

1 2 3 Metres

General arrangement of the Horten Ho 229 V2-1
revised project with 2 Jumo 004 jet engines.

Underside view

Rear

Wire is being used here to form the shape for the internal ducting of the engines.

Nose wheel detail and the starboard engine installation in the H IX V2.

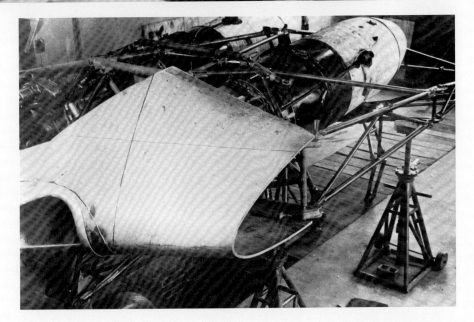

The modified centre section of the H IX V2 incorporating the 'straight' air ducts and empty Jumo 004 engine shells with rotor details absent.

Assembly of the second prototype of the H IX. The engines of the V2 were buried into its centre section in a very tight arrangement, inclined 4 degrees nose-down and splayed 15 degrees outboard. The forward sections of the engines could only be positioned into the forward wing after the removal of the annular starting fuel tanks. Similar to the first prototype, Bf 109 main landing gears were adapted for the H IX V2, with the legs installed this time inclined to compensate for the camber of the wheels.

Right: The centre-section of the H IX V2 after roll out from the assembly shop. Note the Bf 109 main landing gears

CHAPTER FOUR

A Batwing from Gotha City

THE date of 1 June 1944, set for the first flight of the powered H IX prototype, saw the aircraft in the assembly jigs stripped down to its steel-tube frame. In addition to the engineering problems, nearly a week had been lost in May after an Allied air attack which prompted the dispersal of what *Kommando IX* property was possible away from Göttingen airfield. Delays in the H IX programme were apparently confirming Milch's pessimism over the prospects of the Horten jet. At that time, however, the *Generalluftzeugmeister* fell out of Hitler's favour after criticising the *Führer's* intention to convert the Me 262 into a high-speed bomber. The *Führer* wanted a *'Blitz'* bomber first and foremost with which to stop the imminent Anglo-American invasion of France.

Then, on 6 June 1944, the very day the Allies landed on the beaches of Normandy, the Horten project received some unexpected and powerful support. As the war situation became increasingly difficult for the Third Reich, the SS began to move more and more into the centre of power and it even considered the creation of its own air force to be called the *'SS-Flieger'*. Genuine 'total-war' aircraft were being sought, such as the Bachem *Natter*

vertical-launch rocket interceptor and the Horten *Nurflügel* – both promising the 'ultimate' solution for the least possible expense of 'strategic' materials.[22] Following a 15 June 1944 meeting with representatives of the SS, the RLM was quick to order "… off the drawing board" an initial batch of ten H IXs, as was the case with the previously rejected Bachem *Natter*. Close co-operation was established when 30 SS men from the Oranienburg SS Detachment were subordinated to Walter and remained with the Horten *Kommando* until the end of the war.

The initial H IX order, which was later increased to 20 aircraft, went to Klemm Technik in Stuttgart-Böblingen; an additional 20 aircraft had to be produced by the Gothaer Waggonfabrik. Since Klemm was already struggling with the production of the Messerschmitt Me 163B, their Horten order was subcontracted to the large furniture factory May GmbH in Stuttgart-Tamm which had previously produced Klemm Kl 35 wings and wooden parts for the Messerschmitt Me 323. By September 1944 the contract with the Stuttgart group was restricted to the production of H IX wing sets, whereas the assembly of all aircraft went to Gotha.

The Watanzung pressurized flight suit as ground-tested in the H IX V1.

This company had previously produced mixed-construction transport aircraft such as the DFS 230 and the Go 242/244, and was therefore well-suited for the assembly of the H IX. Klemm had constructed the steel-tube fuselage frames for the Go 242/244 since 1940, so there was already a production relationship established between Gotha and Klemm.

During the First World War, the Gothaer Waggonfabrik (a manufacturer of railway rolling stock in Gotha) became famous for its twin-engine biplane bombers G IV to G V, better known as 'Die Gothas'. These aircraft wrought havoc across the English Channel in what were arguably the first strategic air attacks in history. Now the jet-powered Gothas were being devised to bombard England.

Yet it was Gotha which found itself being bombarded. On 20 July 1944 the US Eighth Air Force attacked the Gothaer Waggonfabrik again. The factory was 80 percent destroyed and it never fully recovered by the war's end. As a result, the remaining production facilities were dispersed to several departments in the Gotha area. Apart from Friedrichroda, these were set up in Goldbach, Wangenheim, Luisenthal, Wandersleben, Ohrdruf and in a railway depot of Mitropa AG *(Mitteleuropäische Schlafwagen- und Speisewagen Aktiengesellschaft)* a railway catering firm on the Südstrasse in Gotha.

While the construction of the redesigned H IX V2 had been under way at Göttingen since late June 1944, a group of Horten employees led by chief draughtsman Hans Brüne was detached to

Gotha. There design work started around July 1944 on the production version of the Horten IX, now officially designated '8-229' by the RLM.[23]

The Gotha engineers soon found a number of shortcomings in the Horten design. Their spring catapult-seat, one of the first ejection seats ever conceived, was immediately condemned as unsatisfactory since it provided only 3g of acceleration, and as an alternative a Dornier ejection seat was suggested.

Apart from the ejection seat and the brake chute, another innovation tried during the development of the Horten IX was a pressurised *Watanzug* flight suit made by Dräger in Lübeck. This seemingly futuristic suit, with an outlandish helmet, was to compensate for the lack of cabin pressurisation during high-altitude flights. It was ground-tested in the H IX V1 but was received too late to adapt the H IX cockpit to it, and it was later rejected as impractical.

In September 1944 a commission, comprising amongst others Brüne, the Gothaer chief designer *Dr.-Ing.* Hünerjäger, and *Oberleutnant* Brüning of the *Erprobungsstelle* (E-Stelle, test centre) Rechlin, drew up a list of equipment requirements for the production version of the 8-229 V3.[24] A series of tests was initiated; one of these saw the 8-229 wing manufactured by the company of Robert Hartwig in Sonneberg, undergoing static-load tests in January 1945 at Gothaer's Wandersleben facility. However, ongoing discussions throughout the autumn of 1944 continuously delayed the construction of the 8-229 V3 due to the amount of design changes required.

The head of a pilot would barely fit into the Horten-style cockpit fairing, and some of the instruments could not be seen properly.[25] The installation of the engine, which required partial disassembly and modifications to the standard engine, was considered unsatisfactory as well. The 8-229 V3 was redesigned to accept the production Jumo 109-004B turbojets complete with the standard circular tanks for oil and starting fuel. The entire engine installation was shifted slightly forward. This helped to reduce the necessary ballast. Now the engines protruded through a significant part of the wing surface, necessitating a much more extensive fairing. This in turn allowed reverting to the original 13% wing thickness at the junction with the outer wing panels. Along with the built-in bleed air nozzle cooling system of the Jumo 004B, the flush-mounted steel plates aft of the exhaust were to be cooled by air fed from the lower surface of the wing.

To take the greater gross weight, the landing gear and hydraulics of the 8-229 V3 were completely redesigned with a 1015 x 380 mm nose wheel and the double brake 740 x 210 mm main wheels.[26] The larger nosewheel increased the ground incidence, so that take-off was possible with no or little rotation.

The control system of the V3 was simplified with single-stage brake rudders and elevons with the latter's inner sections now only used as flaps. The rearmost permissible c/g position could only be achieved on the V3 by the addition of 300 kg of ballast weight in the nose.

Since a further lengthy redesign was necessary for the 8-229, it was decided to complete the first three Gothaer prototypes to the V3 standard, in order to provide for a sufficient number of aircraft for the initial flight-test programme.[27] The V3-V5 prototypes were referred to as the *'Göttinger Ausführung'* to distinguish them from the follow-on V6-V15 armed pre-production prototypes. By mid-November 1944 a preliminary description was prepared for the 8-229 V6, embodying all the required modifications. [28]

As the main external difference the V6 was to receive a deeper streamlined underside of the centre section to cover the undercarriage, where the V3 had protruding undercarriage fairings. Although the design of the 8-229 enabled its manufacture by small dispersed factories using unskilled labour, the series version had to be thoroughly redesigned to make it more suitable for mass-production and operations. The hole in the main spar of the centre section was widened and the engines were moved 140 mm outboard to facilitate their easy removal, complete with accessories, from the front. For the same purpose, the axial splay of the engines was cancelled.

The outer wing geometry did not change, but the original extreme Frise-type elevons were found unsuitable for high speed and were replaced by regular blunt-nosed elevons. The 17 mm thick plywood used on the wing's nose was to be substituted by a 15 mm thick composite consisting of two layers of 1.5 mm plywood with a resin-impregnated pressed mix of sawdust and charcoal sandwiched in between. A layered skin of this kind had already been utilized in the construction of the De Havilland Mosquito, with an inner layer made of balsa wood. Since the exotic balsa with a specific weight of circa 100 kg/m^3, (similar to some sorts of modern-day foam plastics), was unavailable to the Germans, a substitute composition of easy-to-find substances was used instead. The purpose of the porous charcoal was to lighten the composite, known as *Formholz*, which otherwise would be almost as dense as a regular plywood (600-800 kg/m^3). Reimar Horten has stated that *Formholz* was "much lighter" than plywood, so the overall weight of the outer wings was reduced by 100 kg.

The c/g problem had to be resolved on the V6 by the installation of an impressive 400 kg of armour plating. Such an armour protection equalled that of the Henschel Hs 129 ground-attack aircraft, while far exceeding that of the *Luftwaffe's* other jets. Its main purpose was to shift the aircraft's inherent aft c/g forward. The pilot's head was to be protected from the front by an armoured-glass plate. The armoured 'bathtub' was to replace the frame structure of the cockpit and the nose-landing gear was to be hinged beneath the 'bathtub'. A mock-up

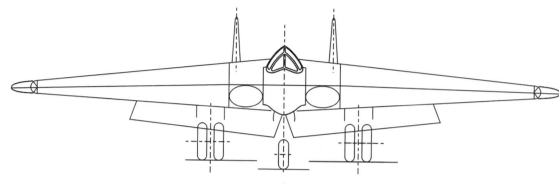

The Lippisch project P.11 started as an enlarged turbojet-powered development of the tailless Me 163 Komet, evolving eventually into an almost-'flying-wing', superficially similar to the Horten Ho 229, but having the vertical empennage. This latter was also to be augmented by the deflecting wingtips.

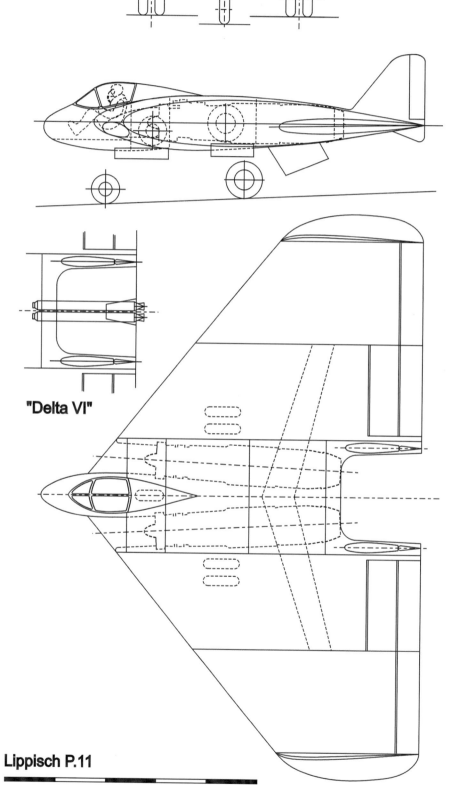

"Delta VI"

Lippisch P.11

Top view

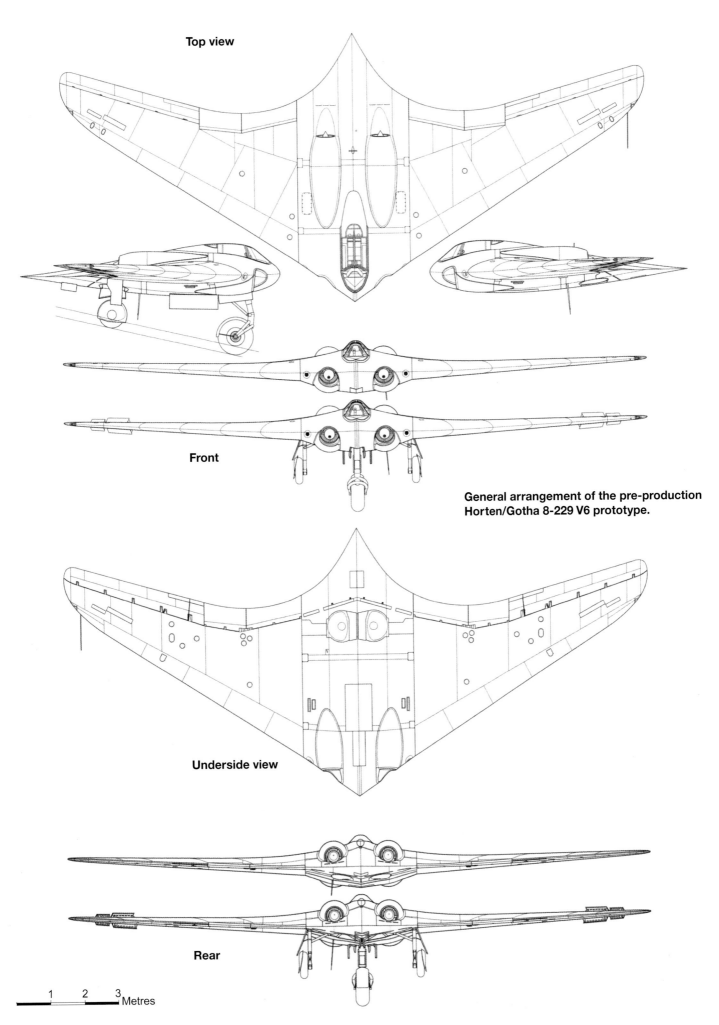

Front

General arrangement of the pre-production
Horten/Gotha 8-229 V6 prototype.

Underside view

Rear

1   2   3
Metres

of the armoured cockpit was built. The GWF designers believed the 8-229 V6 still needed the astounding 600 kg of ballast for what they considered as the minimum permissible margin of longitudinal stability. With fuel tanks empty the c/g moved 6-7% forward. The installation of armament (originally planned for the V3) was to further alleviate the c/g problem. This had been planned to include four 30 mm MK 108 cannon (the total weight of the installation was approximately 360 kg with 90 rounds per gun, excluding the armoured ammunition boxes) or two long-barrelled 30 mm MK 103 (approx. 400 kg with 170 rounds per gun), mounted in the centre section outboard of the engines. The bombload was to comprise two 500-kg calibre bombs carried on the ETC 503 *Wikingerschiff* external attachment pylons. At the same time in mid-November a decision was taken to adapt the 8-229 for the newest Askania EZ 42 *'Adler'* computing sight instead of the previously envisaged Revi 16B.[29] Another advanced aiming/navigational development discussed was the possible inclusion of the K 23 autopilot into the 8-229 control system.[30] Envisaged also were reconnaissance versions of the 8-229 with two MK 108 cannon on the starboard side and various combinations of Rb 20/30, Rb 50/30 or Rb 75/30 cameras on the port side.

However, after the engines of the 8-229 V6 had been moved outboard, it was found that the space remaining between the engines and the root spar was now insufficient for the accommodation of the planned weapons. Placing the cannon in the outer wings would sacrifice the fuel capacity and hence the range, so it was decided to complete the V6-V8 prototypes as reconnaissance aircraft, with a decision on the role of the further prototypes and series aircraft to be taken at a later stage.

Radio equipment was to include the FuG 16zy radio with direction finder, to be later replaced with the newest FuG 15 radio set, the FuG 25a friend-or-foe responder and the FuG 125 blind-landing equipment; the energy was to be provided by a 6 kW generator and a 20 A/h accumulator, and the oxygen by HAS 16 equipment. Cabin pressurization was considered for the production aircraft.

Meanwhile the war situation forced increasingly hectic activity within the RLM, which after Milch's dismissal had been reorganised. Functions of the RLM departments pertaining to military aircraft production had been relegated to the *Reichsministerium für Rüstung und Kriegsproduktion* (Ministry for Armaments and War production) under Albert Speer. Further organisational shake-ups followed on 1 August 1944 with the dissolution of the recently established *Jägerstab* in favour of the newly incorporated *Rüstungsstab* (Armaments Staff), directed by *NS-Hauptdienstleiter* (Nazi Party Leader) Karl-Otto Saur. This attempt to centralise control of the industry was countered on the same day by Göring's order for the establishment of an all-encompassing office of the *Chef der Technischen Luftrüstung* (Head of Technical Air

Armament), or Chef TLR, under *Generalmajor* Diesing. *Oberst* Siegfried Knemeyer was appointed head of the TLR *Entwicklungs-abteilung* (Development Department). Knemeyer had followed the development of the Horten aircraft very closely since he had become a member of Göring's staff in late 1943. Later in mid-1944 he sent his representative to Göttingen to assess the progress of the H IX programme.[31] It was probably around this time that he took the opportunity personally to fly the H IIIe in Oranienburg.

Although the in-service date of the H IX was slipping towards an indefinite future, thought was already being given to the training of the future *Nurflügel* pilots. For that purpose, the very first H IX production order also called for 12 H III trainer gliders. While the May GmbH furniture factory in Stuttgart-Tamm apparently delivered none of these, the Horten Göttingen works produced two H IIIg training tandem-seat gliders in 1944. Flight training commenced from July of that year at the NSFK gliding schools in Klippeneck and Hornberg.

At the same time, a satellite facility of *Luftwaffen-Kommando IX* was established at Hornberg. Amongst the Horten brothers' employees there were their sister *Fräulein Dipl.phys.* Gunilde Horten and Karl Nickel, who was in charge of calculations. In the autumn of 1944 one of the two H IIIg gliders (WNr.31, LA-AI) was converted at Hornberg into a single-seat H IIIh research vehicle. Modifications included installation of a precision angle-of-attack measurement device mounted on a long boom projecting up and forward of the nose, two yaw-sensors and a drogue device for probing into the aircraft's wake. A set of test equipment was fitted behind the pilot, replacing the rear seat. The H IIIh test-flying programme at Hornberg by Herman Strebel probably included investigation of the H IX-type drag rudders, and accumulated in the end some 103 hours. Also used on this aircraft, along with the H IIIf and H IV, was a c/g winch tow technique that was developed at Klippeneck in the summer of 1944.

For advanced and conversion training the two-seat H VII was to be used. After protracted development, the first prototype was finally taken to the air by Walter Horten in May 1944 from Minderheide airfield near Minden. A plan to fit an additional Argus pulsejet engine was again considered and rejected after consultation with *Dr. Dietrich* of Argus, who told Reimar that the pulsejet was too noisy for practical use.[32]

In the autumn of 1944 the H VII was presented at Oranienburg to *Reichsmarschall* Göring in an attempt to fight off the critics of the *'H-Programm'* as the Horten-programme was now classified. The RLM had been investigating the Hortens' activities, wondering about the viability of their building sailplanes concurrently with the Horten IX project; in August/September 1944 an attempt was undertaken to draft the Horten workers for service on the Eastern Front. Concern was expressed about

Oberst Siegfried Knemeyer, head of the TLR Entwicklungs-abteilung, sits on the edge of the cockpit of the H IIIe at Oranienburg in 1944. Sitting in the cockpit is Hptm. Theodor 'Ted' Rosarius, commander of the 2./Versuchsverband Ob.d.L, also known as the Zirkus Rosarius, which was responsible for the operational assessment of captured Allied fighters and acquainting Luftwaffe fighter pilots with them.

the single-engine controllability of the flying wing, taking into account the absence of 'normal' directional controls. In fact, the H VII's ability to fly on one engine had already been confirmed by Scheidhauer in one of the earlier flights. Another flight ended with a successful landing after one of the engines had to be shut down following a propeller accidentally going into reverse. Walter Horten, too, had performed the one-engine-out handling of the H VII at a very low altitude. The asymmetric thrust could be compensated by lowering the wing with the running engine. Sufficient directional control could be maintained even in the landing configuration with flaps down. All this Scheidhauer successfully demonstrated to the *Reichsmarschall*.

By the war's end a second H VII was close to completion at the Peschke works in Minden, together with another 17 or 19 incomplete production examples, re-designated by that time as 8-226 (Ho 226).[33] According to some sources, the third H VII (first production) was nearing completion at Minden, while the complete H VII V2 had been disassembled and stored at the Schwarz Propeller Werke in Eilenburg which later fell into Soviet hands. Unlike the first H VII, production examples received the standard drag rudders, although the sliding bar rudders of the type used on the H VII V1 had been considered for the production version of the H IX. At the request of the RLM, the outer wing flap was locked up on the second H VII and omitted entirely on the production version in order to simulate the higher landing speed of the H IX.

Thanks to the successful presentation to Hermann Göring, the Horten IX escaped the fate of many other aircraft programmes that were stopped

in the autumn of 1944, and the Hortens remained safe to continue with their experiments. The transonic ambition was further pursued, and since model tests showed considerable lift reduction on highly swept wings, another approach was given a try. One of the H II L gliders was modified with a new centre section which was given a sharp sweep angle, so that it formed a pointed nose extension. It was thought that the nose was the first to experience shock waves, so increasing its sweep angle should decrease the overall drag, while the lower sweep of the outer wings would provide for a higher lift at low speeds.[34] Indeed this was a shape of the future, although the slow-flying glider could not validate it. At the same time, simulated air intakes had been arranged which affected the airflow but were different from the H IX V2 design. It is not certain, therefore, what practical results were obtained in these experiments. The long nose obscured a good deal of downward visibility, so Heinz Scheidhauer embarked unwillingly on that 'U-Boot', in mid-1944.

The engineless H XIIIa was tested by Scheidhauer and Herman Strebel at Göttingen in more than 10 flights beginning from 27 November 1944. Tests continued at Göppingen with Herman Strebel at the controls. This glider consisted of H IIIb outer wings attached to a new centre section that provided a sweep angle of 60 degrees. In a total of 10 hours of test-flying the lift coefficient was found to be very low and handling somewhat problematic.

This test bed was followed by the entirely new H XIIIb delta wing design with a leading-edge sweep of 70 degrees. The wing was to have a symmetrical low-drag DVL section, with a maximum thickness at 45% chord. It was thought

The H II L modified for the development of the two-seat H IX derivatives. Note the additional vertical tail surfaces and the air intakes sealed off by the transparent panels.

Scheidhauer's dog, Purzel, flew with him occasionally. Scheidhauer also presented a dog named Vector to Walter Horten and his wife when they married.

G-forces. To this end, Reimar also considered the idea of a pilot being submerged in a water-filled cockpit. Two more H IIIb gliders were modified in 1944 into the prone-piloted H IIIf in view of the possible utilisation in training the H XIII pilots.

The later H X model had the pilot sitting inside a large vertical fin. This design evolution, which saw a type of empennage adopted for the first time on a Horten aircraft, reflected the controversy developing between the brothers. The pure refined flying wing was Reimar's brainchild, slightly less stable than ideal or desirable, but perfectly acceptable for soaring and amateur flying.[35] Walter insisted that a better directional stability was needed for precise gunnery and bombing. He wanted a vertical fin and rudder to be added to the H IX, and the late-war tailed and swept-wing aircraft projects such as the 'Volksjäger' H X and H XIII were mostly Walter's ideas.

Then there was Lippisch's influence. One of his projects under development in Vienna was the P.13a ram-jet interceptor, which Walter's design undeniably resembled. Although the unorthodox cockpit-in-the-fin layout originated from the pre-war French Pa-22 aeroplane by Roland Payen, the overall delta-wing configuration was first realised with Lippisch's DM-1 glider prototype. Later the Hortens denied knowledge of Lippisch's Vienna projects despite the fact that some of Lippisch's models had been tested in the Göttingen wind tunnels in 1943-44 and that Walter had access to almost any research results within the industry.

One of the researches that evoked a great interest in Reimar was the investigation of a laminar flow airfoil that was copied from a wing-root section of a captured P-51D Mustang fighter. This airfoil had produced astonishingly low-drag figures during wind-tunnel tests by the DVL. As the Horten Bad Hersfeld facility had little to do while waiting for the results of the H XIIIa tests, it was only natural for them to just build another glider - an H IV with the Mustang airfoil called the H IVb.

The new wing section was a lot thinner than the original, requiring some structural strengthening. The main spar was laminated with sheet duralumin, and the wing nose was made of 1.8 m-long sections of a ply sandwich with a light *Tronal* filling, a type of resin-impregnated corrugated cardboard. Special attention was given to keep the wing surface as smooth as possible for the laminar section to work; dust covers and gloves were used for ground handling.

Following two test flights by Heinz Scheidhauer at Göttingen in December 1944, the H IVb was transferred to Hornberg for further tests by Herman Strebel. The flying qualities of the H IVb proved disappointing, with a tendency to spin starting at 77 km/h and severe wing flutter setting in at a speed as low as 105 km/h. Both of these faults compounded on 18 January 1945 when the H IVb crashed near Göppingen, killing its pilot Herman Strebel.

that the aircraft, powered with a single HeS 109-011 turbojet or BMW 109-003R combined jet and rocket engine, would penetrate the sound barrier in a dive, and then maintain a speed of Mach 1.4 in level flight. Although a prototype full-size glider was under construction at the Bad Hersfeld facility until the war's end, it seems that the final powered configuration had never been defined. Initial variants envisaged a pilot lying either on his stomach or on his back encapsulated entirely within the wing to lessen drag; an additional advantage of this position was an increased pilot tolerance to the

Just before this tragic end of the project, work had started on a batch of ten H IVb wing sets in the workshop at the Gut Tierstein farm 16 km west of Rottweil. The craftsmen working there had to produce around two wing sets per month in parallel to the usual farm work.

Another attempt to utilise a modified P-51 Mustang airfoil was on the H XII light aircraft which made its sole powerless flight at Göttingen with Scheidhauer at the controls near the end of 1944, and produced almost the same results. This aircraft was distinct from other Horten designs in that it was a side-by-side two-seater with two nose-wheels and one mainwheel, all retractable. This leisure sportsplane, developed under the pretence of being a transition aircraft for the H VII trainer, was destroyed at Kirtorf airfield near Kassel at the end of the war.

While the employees of *Luftwaffen-Kommando IX* worked 90 hours per week to complete the H IX V2, Horten's contribution to the German war effort still was limited mainly to sailplanes. In September/October 1944 the impressive H VI was shipped from Bonn-Aegidienberg to Göttingen. It was planned to demonstrate the high-performance sailplane at Oranienburg before RLM officials to promote the all-wing concept – although only the H IX was actually needed. Danger of flutter restricted Scheidhauer to performing only a few more flights at Göttingen, each lasting 1-1.5 hours to a total of about 10 hours. In the last year of the war he had to take off in darkness for fear of Allied air attacks. Late in 1944 the construction of the second H VI (W.Nr. 34, LA-AL) was started at Bonn-Aegidienberg, then moved to Bad Hersfeld when the Allies were approaching the Hortens' hometown. The glider, of which construction took about 8,000 man-hours, was equipped with a complete oxygen system for record-breaking flying. It was finished just before the end of the war but was never flown.

Walter protested about Reimar's continued work on sailplanes – Reimar argued that all his experimentation was for the sake of the H IX. The truth, as Walter saw it, was that Reimar did not enjoy making warplanes; his greatest ambition was to make the best sailplanes in the world. Reimar admitted later that he preferred building sailplanes because he could produce the complete design himself – managing staff in larger projects was a waste of time to him. And there was a considerable workforce at his disposal, up to 800 people employed at the peak, mostly soldiers who otherwise would be sent to the Front. Also, the numerous dispersed facilities of *Luftwaffen-Kommando IX*, set up to disguise what was happening within the Horten firm from the RLM, helped much in dissipating the Third Reich's dwindling resources. To visit every work site on an average of two times a month Reimar drove thousands of kilometres – exclusively at night in the last months of the war.

Above: The simulated engine compartments of the H II L were essentially the empty air ducts, as can be seen in this photograph taken in a workshop; the rods visible inside are the details of the tubular framework. Note that the lower surfaces of the aircraft remained unpainted but are coated with black primer or covered with black linen.

Downward visibility was marginal on the 'long-nosed' H II L, as can be seen from this photograph.

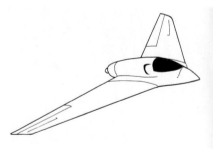

Above: The pointed-nose wing design was utilised later that year when the Hortens prepared their proposal for the Volksjäger ('Peoples' Fighter') competition. This abortive single BMW 003-powered tailless project was designated H X in place of the supersonic project, which was, in turn, redesignated the H XIII.

The Horton H XIIIa.

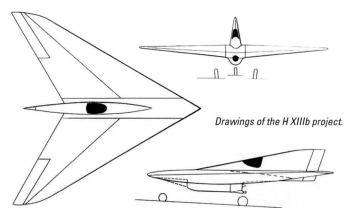

Drawings of the H XIIIb project.

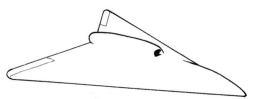

One of the sketches for the proposed Horten supersonic fighter with a prone-pilot position.

Anxious about the half-year lag in the H IX programme, the RLM made an attempt to galvanize the competing Lippisch P.11 project, which actually progressed no better than the Hortens'. A meeting of development programme planners on 21-22 November 1944 proposed that the P.11 would be further pursued in collaboration with the Henschel Flugzeugwerke in Berlin-Schönefeld. Henschel was supposed to build four prototypes designated as Delta VI, but instead by January 1945 the LFW started construction independently in Austria.

Generally very similar to the H IX, the Lippisch design in its final form was a twin Jumo 004-powered tailless fighter-bomber – almost a flying wing but with twin fins on both sides of a trailing-edge exhaust cut-out. The delta-wing had a sweep-back of 37 degrees and a symmetrical airfoil thick enough to accommodate the engines behind the

Models of the H XIIIb project.

Fuel shortages forced the use of oxen as airfield 'tugs' for the H XII.

cockpit, 3,000 litres of fuel and double-wheeled main landing gears. The wingtips deflected downwards to facilitate directional stability, similarly to the fixed *'Lippisch Ohren'* ('Lippisch ears') adopted for the Heinkel He 162 *Volksjäger*. The airframe was of a monocoque construction with a 18 mm *Tronal*-filled plywood skin faced with a 1 mm non-hydroscopic Dynal plastic. Armament was to comprise two 30 mm MK 103 cannon in the outer wing panels, with a provision for two additional MK 103 cannon or one 75 mm BK 7.5 cannon in an external pack.

It was hoped to fly the glider prototype of the Delta VI by March 1945, but in April it was found by US troops in an incomplete state at Ramsau near Salzburg. Two Jumo 004 engines for the Delta VI V2 had been delivered to LFW, but no fuel was available despite the highest priority being allocated to the project.

Meanwhile the second prototype of the H IX was nearing completion at Göttingen. On 17 December 1944 the H IX V2 was delivered to Oranienburg for flight tests – its *'Fledermaus'* ('Bat') appearance caused a sensation amongst the *Fliegerhorst* ground crews.

After Scheidhauer had performed the unpowered maiden flight of the H IX V1 nine months before, another test pilot was being sought to conduct the powered tests. The fact was that *Oberleutnant* Heinz Scheidhauer, although being the most experienced all-wing pilot in the world, did not have an official twin-engine rating. This did not prevent him from flying the twin-engined H VII, but he was not allowed to fly the 7-ton H IX V2.

Reimar wanted Hanna Reitsch to test the H IX – a 'star' pilot who had given a generally positive report on the H II six years earlier. However, she was in Vienna at the time, waiting impatiently for Lippisch's Delta. So the Hortens finally chose *Lt.* Erwin Ziller.

During May/June 1944 Ziller underwent initial all-wing training, performing several flights at Göttingen in H II, H IIIb, H IIIf and H IV sailplanes for a total of about eight hours. His powered all-wing training followed in early December with single H IIId and H VII sorties. He then went to Oranienburg where he accomplished several gliding flights in the H IX V1 (W.Nr.38) on 11, 16, and 22 December, each lasting an average of 20 minutes for a total of about 1.5 hours. Meanwhile the powered V2 was being prepared for its first flight.

Reimar Horten recalled forty years later that he was present for the first flight of the H IX V2 (W.Nr.39), which he thought had taken place about 18 December 1944 before his leave for the Christmas holidays. Erwin Ziller's logbook does not list any flights on that date, although the block of the H IX entries does include a 25- and a 22-minute flight on 23 December 1944. These are different from most of the other glider flight entries in missing the *Ausklinkzeit* (time of release from the tow-plane) data. Yet, this proves nothing in itself, taking into account the general disorder of Ziller's later war logbook. In any case, according to Walter Horten, Ziller made flights that he did not log – although he did log some very short hops, and would hardly miss out the historic first *Nurflügel* jet flight. On the same day, 23 December 1944, a representative from the *E-Stelle* Rechlin reported a first ground engine run on the '229 V2'.[36] Whether this could have been followed by high-speed taxi runs and occasional hops along the runway or even a full flight sequence, is hard to tell definitively – if Reimar would even have allowed Ziller to do this without having undertaken some preliminary jet training.

This training did not take place until a week later, when Ziller performed his first two jet flights in a two-seat Me 262 B, E3+04, of the *E-stelle* Rechlin from Lärz airfield on 29 December 1944. During the two last days of 1944 he flew three solo flights in Me 262 As, E3+01 and E4+E5, for a total of 1 hour 20 minutes. Scheidhauer was supposed to join the test programme later. To obtain the necessary twin-engine rating he was trained by Ziller and Walter Horten on the He 111. Subsequently he often flew this He 111 to tow the H IX V1. Scheidhauer had also been enlisted for, but never entered, the Me 262 training.

Having just started the H IX V2 tests, Reimar interrupted them as he left for Bonn to be with Walter and their parents for Christmas. (There he could also take the opportunity to give some attention to the treasured H VI V2 being

The H VII V1 in a hangar in Göttingen. To the right, the nose of the H IX V1 is visible. Both aircraft wore identical unsophisticated colour schemes.

crafted at Bonn-Aegidienberg). He forbade resumption of the H IX trials until his planned return after New Year's Day. However, other events overtook the Horten brothers and distracted them from the H IX V2 testing.

In fact, the Hortens became involved in yet another ambitious project. Earlier that month, the Horten *Luftwaffen-Kommando IX* at Göttingen had been visited by *Oberst* Knemeyer, who asked the brothers to design an all-wing strategic bomber. By that time, the RLM had renewed its old request for the so-called *'Amerika-Bomber'*, a long-range aircraft capable of delivering a 4000 kg bombload to New York City. Bombing the Manhattan skyscrapers was a dream long-cherished by Hitler; conventional bombs would be deadly enough – to say nothing of the atomic weapon that the Third Reich was endeavouring to develop.

The leading German aircraft companies of Messerschmitt, Arado, Heinkel and Junkers submitted a number of projects including several all-wing proposals to fulfil the requirements. The estimated ranges of the proposed aircraft (and the average service life of existing German turbojets) allowed only for reaching the US East Coast with no chance of returning. Even this would only be possible when starting from airfields in western France, which by that time had already been liberated by the Allies. During the Christmas 'holidays' the Hortens made calculations for ten variants of a flying wing bomber powered by various combinations of Jumo 004, BMW 003 or Heinkel-Hirth HeS 011 jet engines. Finally six Jumos were chosen, buried inside the wing in a layout strongly resembling an enlarged H IX. A rocket-assisted take-off was envisaged with the use of a jettisonable landing gear to save weight, the landing to be performed on some kind of skid or on air bags.

To investigate some basic issues related to the design of a large flying wing, the Hortens decided to build an interim test aircraft based on their H VIII maritime patrol bomber. This early proposal was essentially a double-size H III powered by six

640 hp BMW VI pusher engines, capable of a 20 hour endurance at 500 kp/h. Another project, also designated H VIII, had been contemplated as a 60 passenger transatlantic commercial transport.

The Hortens' lasting interest in large multi-engine all-wing aircraft was logical, since such an aircraft would better realise the advantages of the flying wing, allowing the engines and other components to be buried entirely inside a more slender wing. Furthermore, unlike conventional aircraft, the weight of a flying wing grows proportionally to its area, thus keeping the wing loading within acceptable limits for a large aircraft.

Without official support, the Hortens started to build the H VIII with its 40 metre wingspan and six 236 hp Argus As 10 engines. Alongside the full-scale flight-tests, the aircraft was to be used as a flying wind tunnel for testing the H XVIII models. For this purpose, a giant venturi tube with a 2 x 2.7 m throat was to be placed beneath the centre section. It was expected to obtain an 800 km/h low-turbulent airflow in the throat. The significant airflow turbulence of the German wind tunnels had been a hampering factor in the development of laminar airfoils. Besides, it was thought that cheaper wooden models could be used because of the absence of dust in the airflow. In this way, the big Horten all-wing would be unique in being tested two ways at once, both in full size and in model form.

Reimar had needed a wind tunnel for his research ever since 1934-35, but this had remained largely unavailable to him, leaving the Hortens with their sailplanes to test various design aspects. Tools such as small pieces of paper, wool tufts or a stethoscope attached to the wing surface to investigate the turbulent flow, were all that the Hortens could depend upon – before the H VIII. Instead of the wind tunnel tube, a rear-loading cargo compartment could be suspended with the internal dimensions of 6 x 3 x 4.25 m. Without the external attachments the aircraft could be used for training the future H XVIII crews.[37]

The H IX V2 on the concrete runway at Oranienburg. Although not visible in available photographs, there were no cowlings on the rear parts of the V2's engines, according to some reports. The fire extinguishers standing beside the aircraft were indispensable for the ground test runs of the engines.

These photographs show ground crew helping to hold the H IX V2 on the concrete runway at Oranienburg, while its pilot, Erwin Ziller, sequentially starts the Jumo engines under supervision from a Junkers mechanic.

The H IX V2 in the air.

Fliegerbildschule Hildesheim Aufn Horten

The 'Robot' photo-camera installed on the H IIIb to photograph the wool tufts that visualised the airflow at the wingtip.
The weight and drag of the installation was counter-balanced by the sheet metal at the opposite wingtip. In the same way,
the wool tufts on the white-painted centre section were also photographed in order to investigate the 'Mitten-Effekt'.

CHAPTER FIVE

The Last Stronghold in Thuringia

I N January 1945 Reimar worked simultaneously on the H VIII, H XVIII and H IX projects, shuttling between Göttingen and Bad Hersfeld. The outcome of this activity was not all that positive as the mid-January minutes of the *Chef TLR* related Gotha's complaints that the much-awaited Horten IX (8-229) was still far from series production due to constant design revisions by Horten.[38] Contrary to this, Reimar later claimed that neither he nor Walter had ever approved the changes that Gotha had made to the 8-229 design without consulting them.

Criticism regarding the 8-229 design faults continued to pour in from Gotha ever since their own all-wing projects, designed and tested in the wind tunnel by *Doktoringenieur* Rudolf Göthert, had been rejected in favour of a design created by "amateurs". Having evaluated the Horten drawings, both Göthert and the technical manager of Gotha, *Dr.* Berthold, submitted to the RLM an alternative project called the P-60, which at first they wisely presented as a further development of the 8-229. However, their comparative analysis of late January 1945 pictured a remarkably different design, allegedly far superior to the 8-229.[39]

The Gotha P-60 project incorporated a highly swept wing (47 degrees of quarter-chord line sweep vs. 28 degrees on the 8-229) with a geometrical twist. 13% symmetrical laminar wing sections were used with the maximum thickness point changing from 50% chord at the root to 30% at the tips. Handley Page automatic leading-edge slats were envisaged (these were also considered for possible adoption to the 8-229, but that would never have been approved by Reimar Horten). The lateral and longitudinal control was by means of two-piece blunt-nose Frise elevons. The outer elevon section was linked directly to the pilot's control column, whereas the inner section was driven by servos to facilitate handling at high speeds. Special attention had been given to the problem of longitudinal and directional stability and controllability of the flying wing, which was thought to require the use of some kind of automatic device for artificial stabilisation.[40] A less complicated solution was devised to improve the directional control of the Go P-60 in the form of eight retractable vertical vanes at the wingtips.

The two engines were placed above and below the 'bat-like' rear part of the centre section, thus eliminating the problem of handling the aircraft in case of failure of one of the engines and somewhat improving directional stability. An alternative layout was also considered with both engines beneath the rear part of the centre section; however the Hortens and the DVL pointed to the vulnerability of the lower engine(s) to debris. Gotha argued that the P-60 had a better mass distribution compared to the 8-229. Structurally the centre section was similar to that of the 8-229, while the outer wing panels were made of all-wooden lattice monocoque shells with *Formholz* parts put together with special glue. Such a design offered less weight and a greater fuel capacity. A total of 2,000 kg of fuel was to be filled directly into the outer wings. GWF had been producing similar 'wet' wings for the He 162 and developed a similar design for the 8-229. An additional 1,000 kg of fuel could be tanked in the centre section – unlike the 8-229 where most of its centre section was occupied by the cumbersome landing gear. However, the main landing gear of the P-60 was similarly oversized with adapted Junkers Ju 88 units which bore 85% of the aircraft's weight. The main legs retracted forward into the centre section with the wheels rotating through 90 degrees to lay flat, while the nose gear retracted backwards. Like the 8-229, the Gotha P-60a required some 290 kg of armour to obtain a correct c/g.

The worsening war situation demanded that a two-seat all-weather/night interceptor was needed in the first place. In order to minimize drag a unique layout was devised with a crew of two lying prone side-by-side. The BMW 003 turbojet, already in mass-production, was chosen as the primary powerplant, while the Jumo 004 could be easily adopted as an alternative. Also considered was an auxiliary 2,000 kg-thrust Walter rocket motor. A critical Mach number of about 0.85 was expected, corresponding to a top speed of 900 km/h at 7,000 m.

In March 1945 this configuration was succeeded by the Heinkel-Hirth HeS 011-powered P-60b with a greater wingspan. Further evolution of the project saw the abandonment of the most exotic solutions. Conventional fins and rudders placed between the elevon sections replaced the retractable vanes. The crew was seated in tandem in a conventional pressurized cabin; this layout avoided the need for ballast armour and enabled installation of the ejection seats and the advanced FuG 240 *'Berlin'* radar with a radome-covered dish antenna. When it was realized that neither this equipment nor the Heinkel-Hirth engine would be ripe for series production in the near future, a simplified BMW 003-powered P-60c was proposed. The older FuG 220 *'Lichtenstein'* SN-2 radar was to be installed, combined with the new *Morgenstern*-type dipole antenna partially covered by a plywood nose cone. All of the successive variants were to be armed with four 30 mm MK 108 cannon with 170 rounds per gun or two MK 103 cannon with 175 rounds per gun.

A degree of manipulation of the facts and figures helped Gotha to obtain the RLM's permission to develop the P-60 by 2 February 1945.

With doubts being cast over the future of the H IX, the second prototype was at last cleared for flight after more than a month's idle stay at Oranienburg. On 2 February 1945, the H IX V2 finally took to the air at the hands of Erwin Ziller. According to Reimar and Walter Horten's instruction, Ziller was to make 30-minute flights at 4,000 metres altitude or less, not exceeding 500 km/h indicated airspeed. During the first flight, a speed of 300 km/h was attained with the landing gear down.

The second test flight on the next day ended with a hard landing due to the premature deployment of the brake chute, resulting in damage to the landing gear. The ensuing repair delayed the next flight by two weeks.[41]

According to Ziller's telephone reports to Reimar, the H IX took off with a partial fuel load at a speed of 150 km/h following a ground run of about 500 metres. The estimated rate of climb was about 20-22 metres per second at full throttle, but precise measurements had not been made. Ziller reported that the handling characteristics were as expected except for the marginal longitudinal stability. In contrast to the expected problems, the elevator and aileron control proved sufficient during landing and the landing approach speed was 120-130 kph. The temperature-sensitive paint applied to the decking behind the engine exhausts indicated that the heat levels were within limits. During one of the test-flights Ziller was able to check his H IX against the Me 262 in a joint manoeuvring; the Horten reportedly could out-turn and out-climb that aircraft due to a significantly lower wing loading.

Satisfied with the test reports[42], the RLM confirmed Gotha's order for three *'Göttinger Ausführung'* V3-V5 prototypes and ten V6 – V15 *Zerstörer* prototypes, to be followed by 40 initial production 8-229 A-0 aircraft. At the same time, the H VIII was officially approved. Construction of the first prototype in Göttingen progressed quickly through the spring of 1945, with the maiden flight tentatively planned sometime in November 1945.

Leutnant Erwin Ziller participated in the Eben-Emael operation in May 1940 as a pilot of a DFS 230 assault glider, then served as a glider instructor at Parchim and a factory test pilot at Focke-Wulf. The Hortens respected Ziller very highly both as a pilot and a person.

The search for a suitable site for the construction of the H XVIII Amerika-Bomber continued almost until the end of the war. One such place was the massive concrete production bunker, known as Weingutt II, built in the Iglinger Wald near Kaufering. The 18 metre thick carapace roof was to be covered with earth and trees for camouflage.

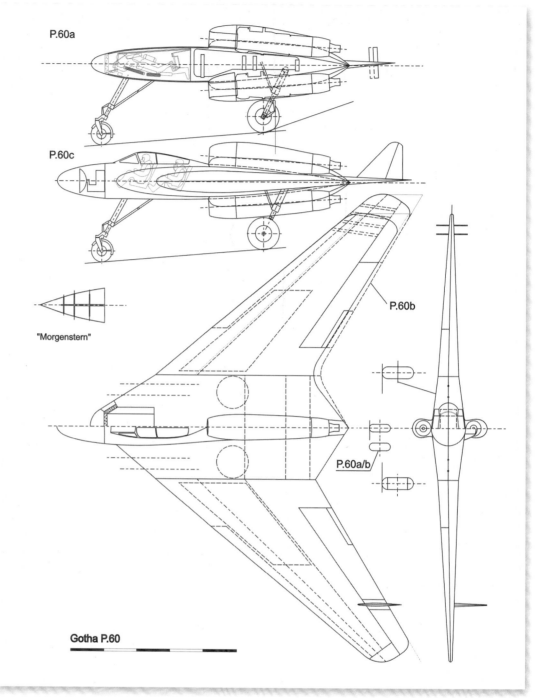

P.60a

P.60c

"Morgenstern"

P.60b

P.60a/b

Gotha P.60

The successive versions of the Gotha project P-60 did inherit some Horten ideas, as evident from their 'bat-tails'. The same construction principles and materials like Formholz were to be utilized. The main external difference was the location of engines and the vertical stabilizers at the wingtips. The aerodynamic layout comprising high wing sweep and symmetrical airfoils was optimised for transonic speeds.

While the Horten team at Oranienburg was busy repairing the bent struts of the H IX's undercarriage, back in Göttingen the Horten brothers were facing double pressure. First, the plans for the H XVIII *Amerika-Bomber* were pushed ahead; even before precise calculations could be made, production of this aircraft was already allocated to a giant underground complex at Kahla. Near this Thuringian town 60 km east of Gotha, a factory known as the *Flugzeugwerke Reichsmarschall Hermann Göring* (REIMAHG) had been under construction since April 1944 in an old kaolin mine beside the village of Großeutersdorf.

The 50 km-long tunnel system was dug under terrible conditions by prisoners from the concentration camps; almost one thousand of them died during one year of construction. The contracted Belgian engineers enlarged the existing tunnel system, creating underground assembly halls up to 15 m wide where the aircraft subassemblies were made. These were then moved outside to the three massive concrete bunkers with up to 3-metre thick walls, where final assembly, painting, and armament firing adjustments took place.

The assembled aircraft were then lifted 100 metres up to the hilltop on a platform along a railed ramp. The hilltop had been levelled off and a concrete runway some 1,500 m[43] long and 30 m wide built, with both 400 m long ends given a slight slope to aid take-off.

The basic aim of REIMAHG was to build 1,000 Me 262s monthly, although only about 20 aircraft were actually completed by the end of the war and the factory itself was about 60-70 per cent completed. The runway length was not entirely sufficient for the Me 262 to take off, let alone for a

long-range bomber. The centre section of the H XVIII could probably only be joined with its wing panels after having lifted them to the 'flat-top', in the open air and under Allied-controlled skies with constant danger from aerial bombardment or strafing. The Me 262s (and possibly the H XVIII) would then be flown to a remote site to be fitted with complete equipment and to undergo final testing.

The wooded hills and valleys of Thuringia were deemed to be the Third Reich's last stronghold in central Germany with which to face the advancing Allied armies. The Chief of the *Rüstungsstab*, Karl-Otto Saur, gave the Hortens 48 hours to move from Göttingen to Kahla, where their activity would be supervised by the *Gauleiter* of Thuringia, Fritz Sauckel[44]. Reimar did not like the order so the company stayed where it was. Indeed neither the schedule nor the overall plan were anywhere close to reality. Furthermore the calculated range was still insufficient for the H XVIII to return home. "Don't worry", said Saur, "We will *retake* France to start closer to America." Around 15 February 1945 Saur repeated his order; Reimar and Walter visited Kahla but decided they could not work "...in a POW environment".

Difficulties were in store for the brothers when Saur summoned both of them to Berlin, yet there was a second problem brewing. On 16 February 1945 a meeting had been held at DVL Berlin-Adlershof devoted to a critical comparison of the 8-229 versus the Gotha P-60 project.[45] The Horten brothers neglected the invitation and did not attend the meeting, choosing instead to present their counter-arguments in writing[46] – to which the GWF readily retorted with their counter-counter-arguments.[47] This criticism compounded the same day with a report on faults discovered during inspection of the 8-229 V6 mock-up.[48]

Without proper defence on behalf of the 8-229, it came as no surprise that the RLM was increasingly inclined towards the P-60 – based on figures prepared by Gotha. One particular shortcoming of the 8-229 design emphasised by the critics was the fact that it was not possible, without

a major redesign, to exchange the Jumo 004 engines for the more powerful, yet larger Heinkel-Hirth HeS 109-011 engine which was under development at the time.

Addressing the critics and the growing need for a night interceptor, the Hortens prepared in February 1945 a two-seat version of their fighter designated H IXb.[49] The Hortens' in-house documents also referred to this project as the H IX V6. The Hortens had retained their own *Versuch* (prototype) numbering independent from GWF, which caused considerable confusion in later references.

The H IXb project envisaged modification of the production 8-229 with a 1 metre long extension to the nose of the centre section to make room for an extra crew member. The crew was seated in an armoured tandem cockpit; the all-weather/night fighter version was to have the latest FuG 244 '*Bremen*' radar with a dish antenna. Another internal Horten project was the two-seat H IX V7 trainer. Ultimately, the proposed two-seat H IXs would probably have needed some kind of vertical stabilizer since the extended nose, while resolving the c/g problem, further degraded the directional stability of the aircraft.

The Red Army was already on the banks of the River Oder some 80 km east of Berlin, preparing for its final assault, when Erwin Ziller boarded the H IX V2 on 18 February 1945. His thoughts were far away since just before the flight he received a message that his family, including his baby son, whom he had not yet seen, were fleeing as refugees from the Russians.

In accordance with the test programme, a maximum rate of climb and speeds at altitudes up to 4,000 m had to be ascertained during the third flight. Shortly before that flight, a FuG-15 radio had been installed in the aircraft, but communication with the tower was not established. The weather was overcast with a low cloud base at about 500 m, but in the afternoon the amount of sky covered had decreased to about 6/8, enabling Ziller to take off at 14.15 hours. Ascending at about 35 degrees the

The H IX V2 taxiing for take-off. The presence of the Morane-type antenna suggests that the photograph was taken on, or shortly before, 18 February 1945. Note in the background a Kettenkrad half-track usually used for towing aircraft and ground equipment. Less than an hour after take-off on 18 February 1945, the ground crew chief, Walter Rösler, the last man to see Erwin Ziller alive, was first to arrive with this truck at the crash site.

Walter Rösler.

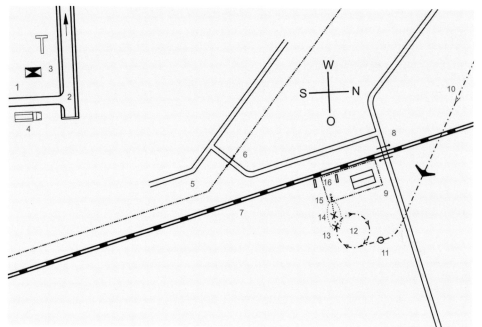

A sketch of the H IX V2 accident on 18 February 1945 near Oranienburg airfield as reproduced from a drawing by Walter Rösler of 7 August 1984. 1: Taxiway; 2: Runway, take-off heading to the west; 3: Ground crew wagon, the observation point of Walter Rösler; 4: Fire engine, arrived at the crash site; 5: Airfield hedge; 6: Airfield gate; 7: Railway; 8: Railway crossing; 9: Home and garden of the railway crossing serviceman; 10: Descent path of the H IX V2; 11: Point of undercarriage lowering; 12: Aircraft circling; 13: Point of hitting the ground; 14: Secondary hitting point and area of debris. Despite the fact that the aircraft was totally destroyed, there was neither an explosion nor fire; 15: Body of Erwin Ziller; 16: Aircraft's engines lying on the railway embankment.

aircraft flew through a clearance in the clouds and disappeared. Ziller made three passes along a pre-defined path south of the airstrip for a team from the *Erprobungsstelle* Rechlin to measure speed and altitude using a theodolite. A speed of 795 kph was measured visually through openings in the clouds; the observed altitude never exceeded 2,000 metres. After about 45 minutes the aircraft emerged from clouds north of the airstrip at an altitude of some 800 m descending in a south-east direction with the right engine dead. The pilot apparently attempted to restart the engine by airflow, diving and pulling up the aircraft several times, descending to 500 m in the process. At a distance of around 1,300 m from the starting place the aircraft took a right turn towards the airfield. Following that, at an altitude of about 400 m, the landing gear was lowered prematurely, leading to a rapid loss of airspeed due to the increased drag. Since the hydraulic pump was normally driven by the now dead right engine, the undercarriage and flaps were extended by the emergency compressed air system and could not be retracted again.[50] The fact that both the undercarriage and the landing flaps were lowered simultaneously was intended and had been designed by Reimar Horten in order to aid the pilot in case of an emergency. However this design feature instantly produced a large amount of additional drag and probably worked against the pilot in this case. An abrupt increase in the engine's noise indicated the pilot's attempt to gain airspeed, flying another 15-20 metres straight. However, the greater asymmetric thrust was countered by a fully deployed rudder, and this led only to a further increase in drag. Having failed to gain airspeed, the aircraft entered a wide right-hand circling turn at a 20 degree bank. Following a full 360 degree turn the pilot seemingly tried to lower the aircraft's nose, while circling continued with increasing bank. At the beginning of the fourth circle the aircraft struck the ground at an angle of about 35 degrees, fifty metres from a railway embankment. On impact both of the engines and the pilot were thrown from the aircraft onto the embankment and an adjoining garden, belonging to a serviceman of a nearby railway crossing. Ziller hit a large tree in the garden and died at the age of thirty-nine years.

Altogether about two hours of flying had been accumulated by the H IX V2. Although Walter did oversee the Horten IX operations in Oranienburg, it appears that, due to a strange coincidence, neither of the Horten brothers ever witnessed their only jet flying.

Walter believed that problems with the engine caused fumes to enter the cockpit, which rendered Ziller unconscious. Walter recalled his dogfight with a Hurricane; its American pilot was dead or unconscious as the damaged fighter made the same wide circles as the H IX V2 had done just before crashing. This might also explain why Ziller did not attempt to bale out; his harness was found torn but not unfastened, and the ejection seat had not been activated. A modified catapult seat propelled by a pyrotechnic ejection device taken from the Focke-Wulf Ta 154 was tested by Gotha the same month with satisfactory results – a dummy was ejected with an acceleration of 13g,[51] – but it was obviously too late for Ziller.

The Jumo engines of the H IX sometimes stalled during start and Junkers mechanics could not provide an explanation for this[52]. Nevertheless, the programme as a whole was not questioned. It was thought (and actually confirmed by the last flight) that the location of the engines close to the c/g provided for acceptable single-engine handling.

In the five days following the H IX V2 crash, the *Luftwaffen-Kommando IX* Oranienburg facility was dismantled and its crew and equipment returned to Göttingen. The last Horten personnel hurriedly left Oranienburg aboard the Scheidhauer-flown He 111, thus escaping enlistment into an airfield defence detachment.

The H VII was also flown to its home base by Scheidhauer. During landing, the undercarriage failed to lower due to a failure of the hydraulics. The aircraft was damaged in the ensuing belly-landing and was not repaired before the end of the war. Walter Horten and Scheidhauer had flown the H VII for a total of approximately 18 hours each.

A wartime illustration of the proposed Horten H XVIIIa.

Below: A poor-quality copy of the photograph from the report on testing the Schleudersitz (catapult seat) of the 8-229, carried out between 13-16 February 1945 at Gotha's test facility 'Abtl. 2296'. The original catapult seat mark 8-229.16Z01 was equipped with a pyrotechnic ejection device 8-154.1101-06A developed for the Focke-Wulf Ta 154 and installed on the launch rail system 8-229.12-10Ho. Seen in the photograph is the catapult seat system mounted in the anchored centre section framework of the 8-229 prior to the test. Immediately after the upper rollers of the seat left the rails during the ejection test sequence, a coupling device immediately behind the headrest engaged a cable that applied a 500 kg backward-directed load to the seat to emulate the drifting effect of the airflow. The upward-angled cable tied to 300 kg counterweight via a pulley would suspend the seat upon ejection to prevent it from damage on falling on the ground. (Seat weight was 17.6 kg plus ejection device of 5.8 kg plus wooden dummy of 100 kg including 25 kg placed on the seat's footrests to imitate the pilot's feet). In the course of the tests the seat was ejected successfully with an acceleration of 130 m/s² (approx.13 g).

Around this time, the H IX V1 made its last flight under the control of Siegfried Knemeyer, who crashed it on landing, causing damage to the landing gear. The glider was brought to Göttingen at the end of March or beginning of April and then transported by train to Brandis airfield near Leipzig,[53] where the Me 163-equipped 1./JG 400 had been stationed since June 1944. The H IX V1 had completed about 40 flying hours in the year since its construction, 30 hours in the hands of Scheidhauer, the rest by Walter Horten and Ziller. As a point of comparison, Scheidhauer had flown the H IV glider alone for up to 50 hours per month, amassing 500 flying hours towards the end of the war. It transpired that the test pilot of the H IX V2, although being an excellent pilot, had the least all-wing experience of all *Luftwaffen-Kommando IX* pilots and only very basic jet training.

A decision was taken that the H IX V1 glider prototype was to be used for training pilots of 1./JG 400 in view of a planned re-equipment of this *Geschwader* with the production Ho 229 and transition trainer Ho 226 (H VII).[54] A plan existed to move the whole Horten IX project to Brandis, but the damaged H IX V1 was never repaired. Nevertheless, some of the Me 163 pilots had already acquainted themselves with the Hortens' *Nurflügel* in 1943 at Bad Zwischenahn where the two H II L gliders were used for transition to the tailless aircraft. This small episode, in the end, would represent the Hortens' only contribution to the German war effort, apart from their participation in the preparations for the abortive 'Operation Seelöwe'. None of the Horten aircraft was ever fitted with armament.

Having nine victories on its record for the cost of 14 aircraft, of which only five were lost in combat, 1./JG 400 needed a more reliable aircraft; replacements such as the Me 263 (Ju 248) and He 162 were considered. It should be noted that Scheidhauer, having flown the Me 163 as a glider, reported that this aircraft was more manoeuvrable and handled better than the H IX; Walter also flew the *'Komet'*, and Reimar admired this Lippisch design. Another *Luftwaffe* fighter unit, 1./JG 54, was scheduled to engage British airfields with the Ho 229 in August or September 1945.[55]

By late February a date of the series production of the Ho 229 still was not foreseeable, and its re-classification as a *Kampfjäger*, an all-weather fighter-bomber, did not speed up development either.[56] To devise new wonder-weapons amidst the catastrophic war situation, or to devote all remaining resources to production of existing high-performance aircraft like the Me 262, was still a matter of a dispute between the *Rüstungsstab* and the *Chef TLR*. Although the Allied forces were closing in on almost every front, an offensive approach was still considered viable and the long-range bomber concept was again pursued. The SS was obviously enchanted with the idea of transatlantic raids, aimed at terrorising the civil population of America and in deterring the USA from further com-mitment to the war.

On 25 February 1945 before a conference in Berlin of the competing aircraft companies par-ticipating in the *Amerika-*

This page and opposite page top - the proposed Horten H XVIIIb.

Bomber projects, the Hortens presented their H XVIII project.[57] Two weeks later, the Hortens were summoned to report personally to Göring who ordered them to proceed with the project in collaboration with Junkers.[58] The latter had proposed an outwardly similar EF.130 all-wing project. A few days later they were joined by representatives of Messerschmitt for a two-day meeting during which it was proposed to modify the H XVIII with a large vertical tail to overcome the expected directional control problems. The six 1,100 kg-thrust Junkers Jumo 004H engines were to be grouped in two nacelles beneath the wing on both sides of the bomb bay outside the main landing gears. A defensive armament was envisaged consisting of two remote-controlled 30 mm MG 213s in the tail and two fixed MG 213s in the nose. It was hoped that the 44-ton aircraft would attain a maximum speed of 900 kph and have a range of 9,000 km.[59] Not satisfied with the proposed configuration, Reimar sketched a new version of a 33-ton flying wing bomber designated the H XVIIIb. Instead of the loathed vertical fin that Reimar thought would create excessive drag, the aircraft acquired two equally ugly under-wing pylons, each carrying two 1,300 kg-thrust Heinkel-Hirth HeS 011 engines. A fixed multi-wheel landing gear was to be mounted under each pylon, to be covered by doors during flight.

The meeting with *Reichsmarschall* Göring, who undoubtedly favoured the Horten brothers, suddenly found them placed ahead of their influential opponents. Until then, the RLM preferred the Gotha concept, and significant progress had already been made on the P-60 project. But at a conference on 12 March 1945 at Göring's Karinhall estate, it was decided that the Horten concept was the only solution for a successful *Nurflügel* aircraft and that the brothers should therefore receive all support to bring their aircraft into production. For that reason the *Chef TLR* was to consider the immediate inclusion of the Horten development work into the *'Führer-Notprogramm'* (the *Führer's* Emergency Programme). A group of specialists was to be organised to collaborate with the Horten brothers, who were to be consulted in every flying wing project. Discussion over the Gotha P-60 flying wing thus ended abruptly, and the project was discontinued.

A final contract worth 500,000 *Reichsmarks* was granted to the Hortens on 23 March 1945 for the development of the H XVIII *Amerika-Bomber*.

As Gotha proceeded throughout March 1945 with the Ho 229, some further variants of the H IX were studied by the Hortens. Apart from Reimar's H IXb, Walter prepared his own *tailless* concept labelled the H IXc. This swept-wing H XIII development represented a dramatic departure from the 'pure' flying wing. The excessive thickness of the flying wing profile precluded achievement of high critical Mach numbers, thus effectively limiting the flying wings to subsonic speeds. Although the Hortens had criticised, on the grounds of their H XIIIa experience, the highly swept wing of the P-60, the H IXc received a sharp 45 degrees sweep of the wing leading-edge and a short root chord. The Jumo 004 turbojets were moved beneath the wing, while the cockpit was placed, similar to the H XIII, inside the large fin. Armament was the same as proposed for the 8-229, comprising four 30 mm MK 108 cannon and a 2,000 kg bombload. Performance estimates were as optimistic as ever: a range of 4,000 km with a top speed of 1,100 km/h.

The Hortens calculated that the Ho 229 V2 and V3 initial prototypes had top speeds of 950-977 km/h. For the V6, their top estimate was 920 km/h (700 km combat range, with a 2,000 kg bombload). Ziller, however, thought the V2 was capable of only 900 km/h. As a point of comparison, the Me 262 fighter powered by the same engines, but having a higher critical Mach number (0.82), could develop only 875 km/h at 6,000 m.

Taking into account the lower drag coefficient of the flying wing, GWF hoped for the 8-229 V6 to obtain 840 km/h at 3,000-4,000 m (830 km/h at sea level, 780 km/h at 11,000 m). DVL expected the same. An independent study by the Henschel company indicated a top speed of 870 km/h for the V2, and data for the V6 close to the above mentioned. Actually the polished V2 developed just below 800 km/h. Other performance figures also dropped when compared to the original estimates: an initial rate of climb of 15 m/s (Me 262: 20 m/s) and a maximum ceiling of 10,000-12,000 m. The maximum range with 2,000 kg of fuel was 1,400 km at 12,000 m (at 100 % thrust).

Reimar admitted in a post-war article that "...in fast flight, the flying wing is only superior to a conventional aircraft, when wing-loadings are equal" [60]. However, the flying wing almost inevitably possesses lower wing-loading as compared to a conventional aircraft of the same gross weight. With this in mind and with conventional jets achieving the performance goals for the H IX by 1950, Reimar preferred to stress the importance for a fighter aircraft of such characteristics as manoeuvrability, high ceiling and low landing speed, all of which the low wing-loading offers.

The Ho 229 needed a 1,100 m airstrip for take-off, which was significantly less than the Me 262 required. The few airfields in Germany that could accommodate the Me 262 were bombed out by the Allies, whereas the Ho 229 could fly from conventional grass airfields thanks to its low wing loading.

Potentially, the production Ho 229 series could combine the speed and firepower of the Me 262 with the long range of the Ar 234. Utilisation of non-strategic materials was equally important,

although this added to the aircraft's empty weight. In any case, the Horten team had virtually no experience in all-metal aircraft construction.

In March 1945 the downfall of the Third Reich was in sight; that month the Eighth Air Force dropped a greater tonnage of bombs on Germany than it had over several previous months combined. All the Reich's oil and coal fields had fallen to the Allies, so not even synthetic fuel could be obtained any more. On 17 March, *SS-Gruppenführer* Hans Kammler became the *'Reichssonderbevollmächtigter der Raketenwaffen und TL-Jäger'*, receiving full power to supervise the development of rockets and jet aircraft. Soon thereafter, he decreed that only production of the Me 262 was to be continued, hence ending all other developments including the Ho 229.

Artists impression of how the Ho 229b may have looked, if it had been built and a FuG Bremen 0 radar had been fitted. As far as is known, no original drawings of this configuration were ever made. Only one prototype of this 5km range radar was completed by the cessation of hostilities in Europe

CHAPTER SIX

Reaching Enemy Soil

A T the same moment the Horten brothers were chosen to invent one last miracle weapon with which to save the Fatherland, their own parental home was being searched by the enemy. Between 11 and 14 March 1945 a joint British-American Combined Objectives Sub-Committee (CIOS) intelligence team inspected the Horten family house in Bonn. There they found a number of design documents and models of the Horten I to XII, which were handed over intact by Franz Berger. Berger had been working with the Hortens since the early days of their career in the late 1920s, at first as a voluntary helper in building the H I and H II, and later as a civil employee of the *Sonderkommando LIn.3*. He had returned from Göttingen about a month before Bonn was overrun by Allied forces to help his family who had suffered in a bombing raid. His willingness to co-operate convinced the CIOS team that he had been secretly entrusted by the Hortens to make contact with the Allied authorities, in the hope of continuing the brothers' work after the war.[61] In fact, Berger carried a mission confided to him by Reimar without Walter's knowledge. He showed Gunilde Horten the following message from Reimar:

'Top secret! Tell to nobody else! Not even Walter knows of this message! The war is lost and in a short time Allied forces will occupy Germany. As soon as this happens, try to reach their people in command and tell them all about our research, the locations, the people, the aircraft. By this way, it is hoped that they will take things over so quickly that nothing is destroyed. It is to be hoped that they then will continue with our development and let us carry on with our research!' [62]

One of the projects that Reimar hoped to continue after the war was a series production of the H IIIe single-seat motor glider, aimed, alongside the two-seater H XII, at the post-war civil market. According to Reimar, a series of 50 H IIIe had been ordered by the RLM from Klemm. It was felt that this VW-powered aircraft could make a very economical trainer. In practice the Hortens organised the final assembly of the H IIIe at the Hornberg gliding school, where the NSFK also produced wings for the He 162. The tubular frames were made by a machine shop at Tübingen, while the all-wooden outer wings were supplied by the Schmidt furniture factory at Donzdorf near Göppingen. Twelve finished H IIIe wing sets were burnt there on 15 April 1945 as the Allied forces approached. Even before Hornberg airfield was destroyed by a rocket bomb attack on 16 April, the NSFK authorities had evicted the Horten subsidiary from the main hangar. The H IIIf, H IIIh, and H IV gliders had been evacuated to the Gut Tierstein farm, while a Fieseler Fi 156 Storch tow-plane was flown to Göttingen. One remaining Horten glider, possibly the H IV W.Nr. 24 which had had its wings clipped after being damaged in an accident, was destroyed before the arrival of US troops. According to Reimar, the H XIIIa that had been tested at Hornberg was later destroyed by the liberated Soviet POWs.

Another commercial project for the post-war Horten Flugzeugbau was the H XIV sporting sailplane, designed along the pre-war Olympic Games specifications. The brothers could, of course, not predict that sport gliding would be forbidden in Germany until 1951, nor that the pre-1940 idea of including soaring in the Olympics would not be revived. As if a most valuable item, the almost complete H XIV was evacuated by the Hortens to Leipzig-Brandis airfield after US troops neared Göttingen in late March 1945. The commander of JG 400, *Hauptmann* Wolfgang Späte, a prominent glider pilot who had won the 1938 Rhön competition, welcomed the sporting sailplane at the military airbase, although his unit was disbanded the same month without using a Horten flying wing for training purposes.

Before long, both American and Soviet troops drew close to Brandis, forcing the Horten employees to flee to the west with the precious H XIV towed in a trailer. Despite all efforts, the glider was later found and destroyed by the Americans.

The Horten brothers themselves left for Berlin, where on 1 April 1945, the H XVIII *Amerika-Bomber* was ordered into production by Kammler despite his own decision two weeks before. After meeting with Saur on the same day, Reimar went to Nordhausen to assess the possibility of setting up the H XVIII assembly line at the giant underground factory at *'Mittelbau Dora'*. Here in the Thuringian Harz mountains Reimar was picked up by Americans on 7 April 1945. Before his arrest Reimar had destroyed some of the Jumo 004 documents he was carrying. The Americans took Reimar by jeep to Göttingen, which was occupied by the US Army on 7 April 1945, the same day that Walter was arrested in Göttingen. Four days later, the Horten brothers were sent to a POW camp at Braunschweig where they spent three days before being transferred to a POW camp at Wiesbaden.

At Göttingen troops of the US 8th Armored Division found the intact H IV (W.Nr. 25, LA-AC)

The H IVa glider being towed behind a Henschel Hs 126.

and the damaged H VII V1. Half-completed H VIII sub-assemblies were found still in their jigs, including the tubular frameworks of the centre section and the wind tunnel venturi tube. Furthermore, a complete set of engines with bearing frames, parts of the fuel system and the landing gear were in the stores. Also found at the *Luftwaffen-Kommando IX* headquarters was a H IX model, but no drawings were found in the completely shattered drawing office. The H VII V1 was later destroyed by the Americans. The H VI V1 glider was recovered near the city and destroyed by the British in August or September 1945.

Meanwhile on 4 April 1945, the US Third Army, advancing toward Leipzig, took the town of Gotha. Kahla surrendered to US forces on 12 April 1945. Friedrichroda was seized on 14 April 1945 by elements of the US Third Army's VII Corps. There they found the almost complete 8-229 V3 without outer wing panels, the skinless centre section of the V4 with its engines and most of the systems installed, and the steel frame of the centre section of the V5. There were also parts and materials in storage for the initial run of 20 aircraft. Of the 20 sets of 8-229 wings that had been ordered in 1944 at May GmbH in Tamm, only one set was said to have been finished by the year's end, but never delivered to Friedrichroda. One 8-229 wing set was reportedly retrieved by the US Air Disarmament Division, Ninth Air Force Service Command (AFSC), at an unspecified location some 120 km from Friedrichroda *"... in a satisfactory condition needing only to be attached to the body"*. The same report mentioned *"...two German engineers who ... expressed themselves as being willing and eager to follow the planes back to Wright Field in order to see their work brought to a successful conclusion."* [63] The two engineers were probably the Horten brothers who were at the time being interrogated by the Allied authorities, while the place where the wings were found could have been the Robert Hartwig Company in Sonneberg.

Continued on page 104

The Ho 229 V3 as found by the Americans at the GWF plant in Friedrichroda. In the background can just be seen what appears to be the framework of the Ho 229 V5. The plywood skin was fixed to the frame by screws, the rows of screws were then sealed off with a fabric strip and painted to protect them from corrosion.

Details of the air intakes and oil tanker/cooler of the Jumo 004 engines.

Details of the landing gear of the Ho 229 V3 as found at Friedrichroda.

Detail view of the tubular centre section and the two installed Jumo 004 engines of the Ho 229 V4. Note the close proximity of the two Jumos to the cockpit.

A US Army Sergeant examines the tubular framework of the 8-229 fifth prototype. This structure had only minor differences to that of the V3 and the V4.

The cockpit of the 8-229 V3. The left nose-section of the skin is missing. The instrument panel was made of thick plywood.

Top View

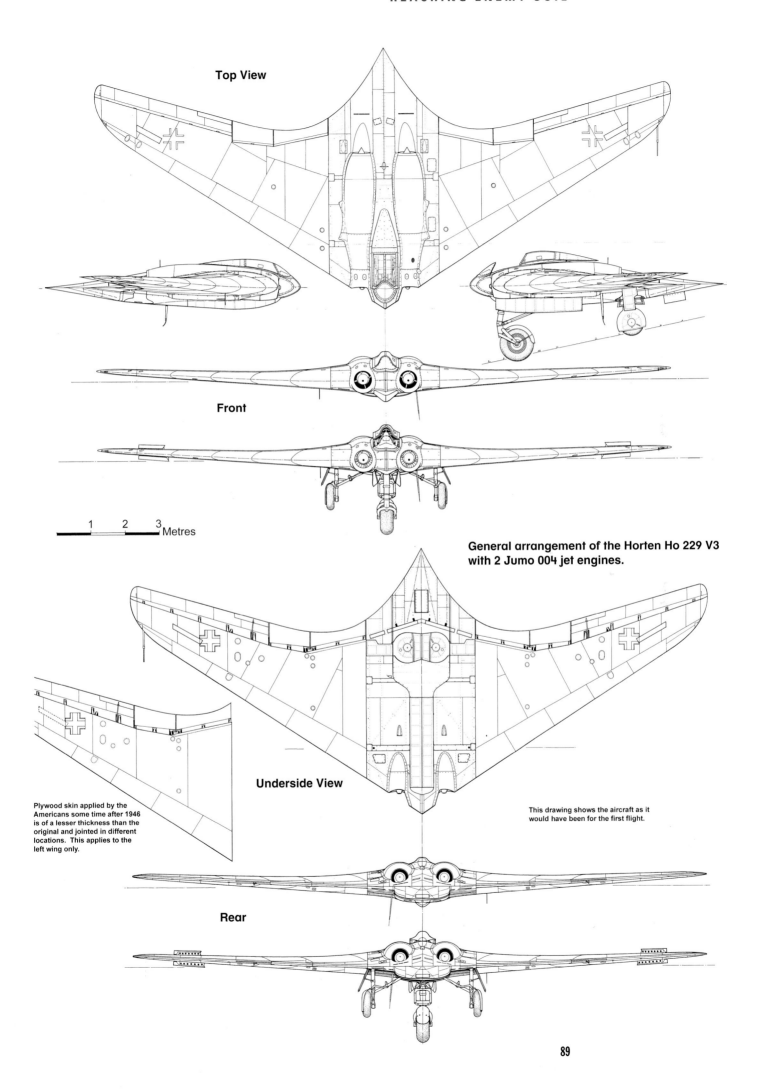

Front

1 2 3 Metres

Rear

General arrangement of the Horten Ho 229 V3 with 2 Jumo 004 jet engines.

Underside View

Plywood skin applied by the Americans some time after 1946 is of a lesser thickness than the original and jointed in different locations. This applies to the left wing only.

This drawing shows the aircraft as it would have been for the first flight.

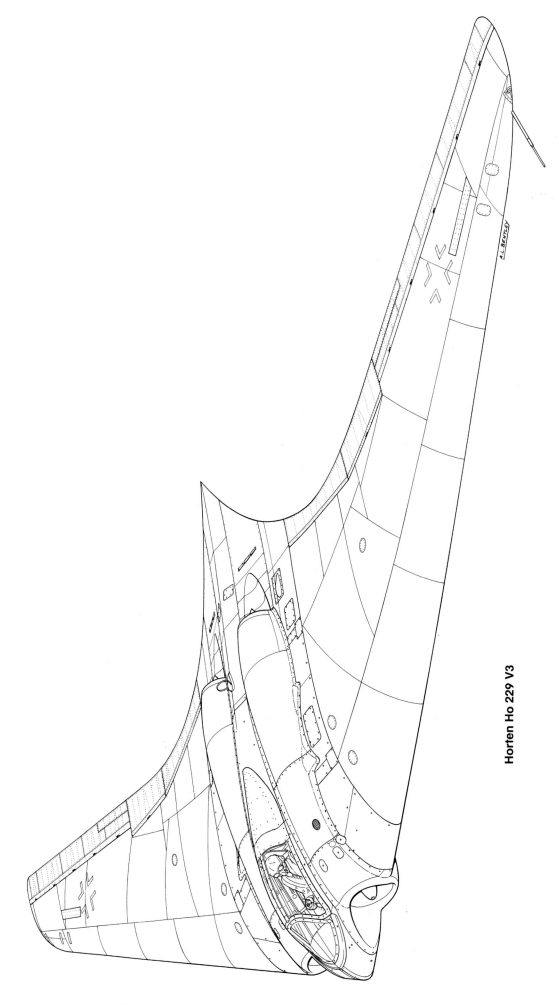

Horten Ho 229 V3

A.L. BENTLEY

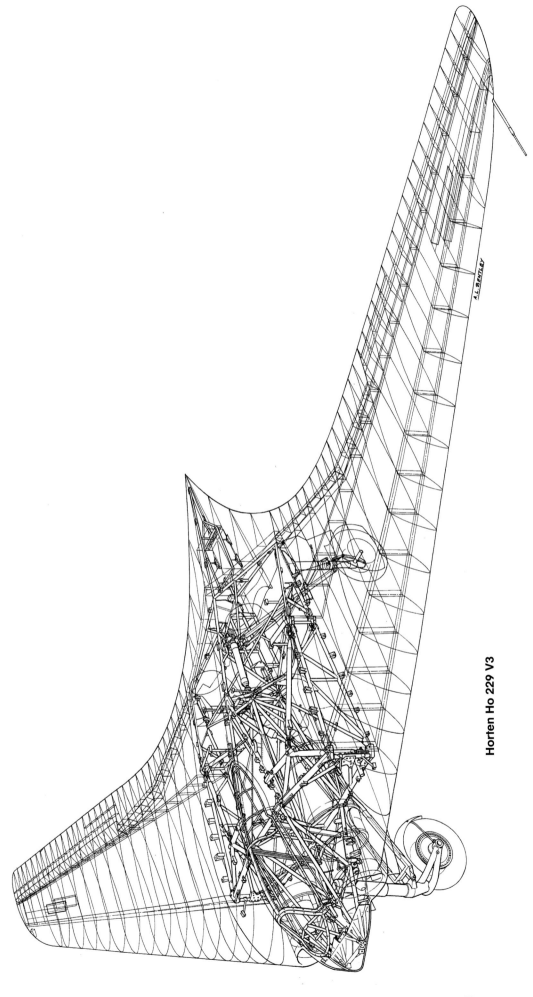

A.L. BENTLEY

Horten Ho 229 V3

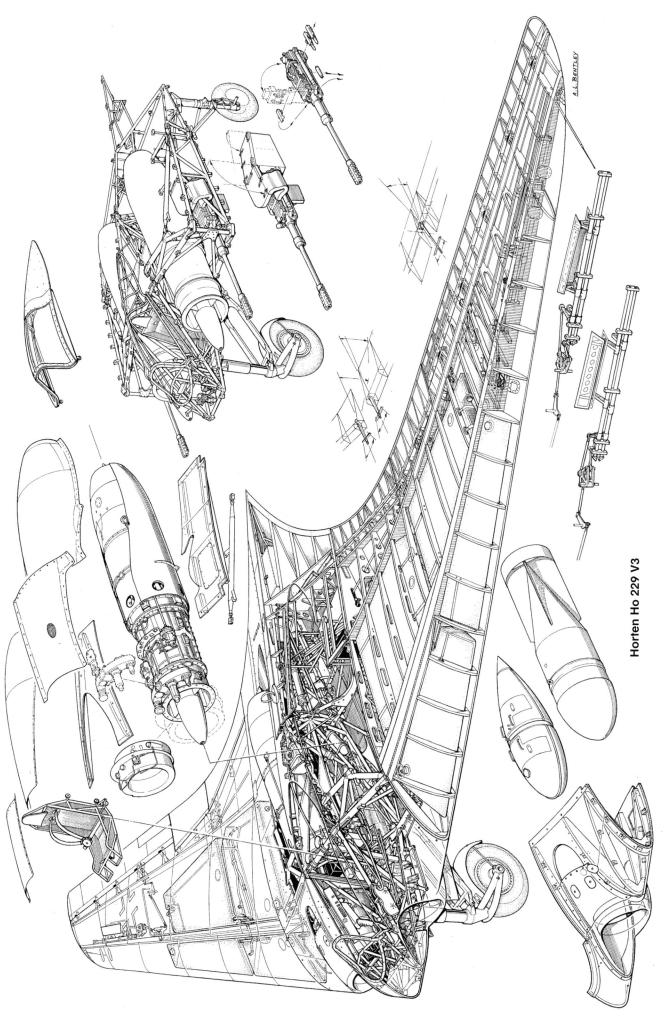

Horten Ho 229 V3

A.L. BENTLEY

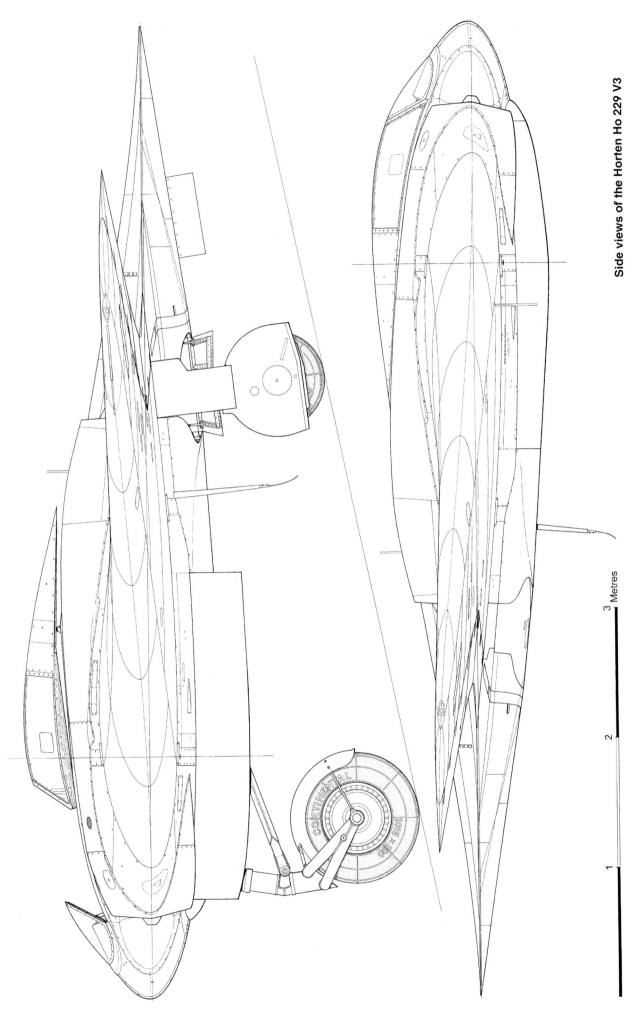

Side views of the Horten Ho 229 V3

3 Metres

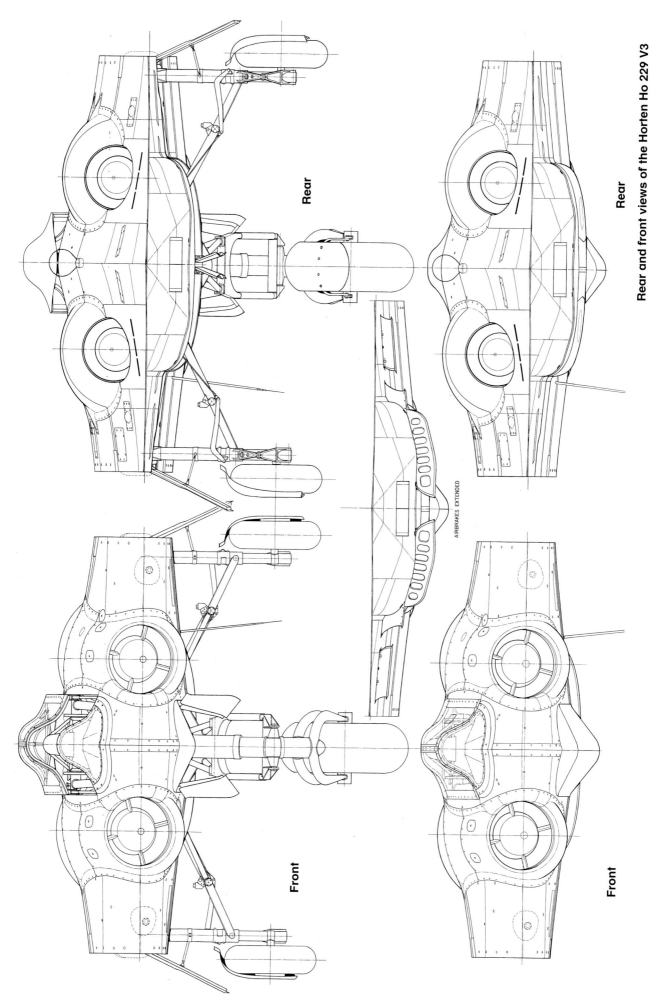

Rear

Front

Rear

Front

AIRBRAKES EXTENDED

Rear and front views of the Horten Ho 229 V3

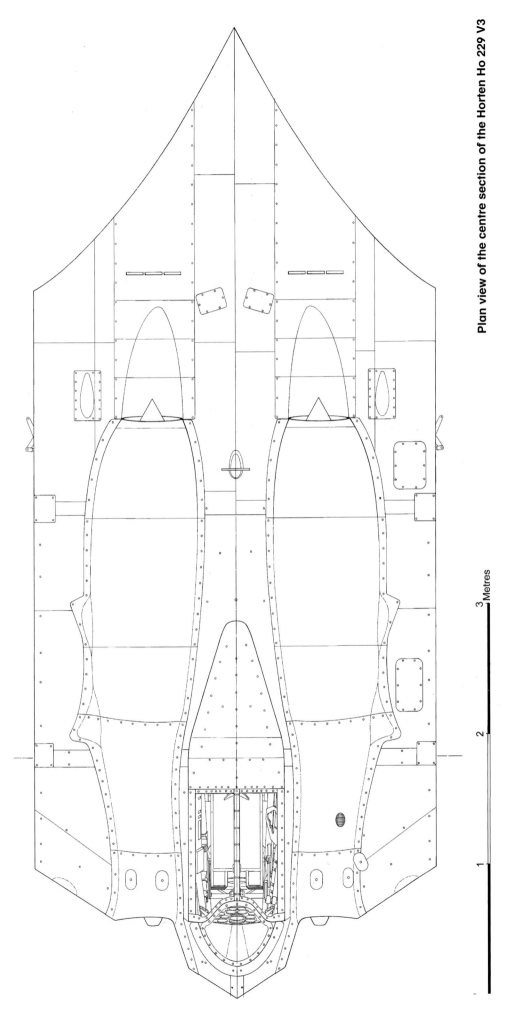

Plan view of the centre section of the Horten Ho 229 V3

3 Metres

2

1

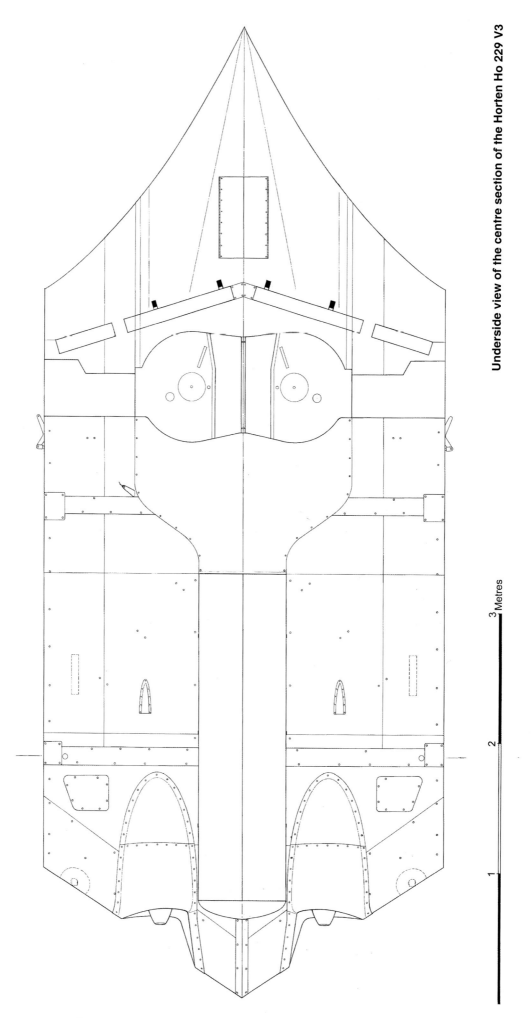

Underside view of the centre section of the Horten Ho 229 V3

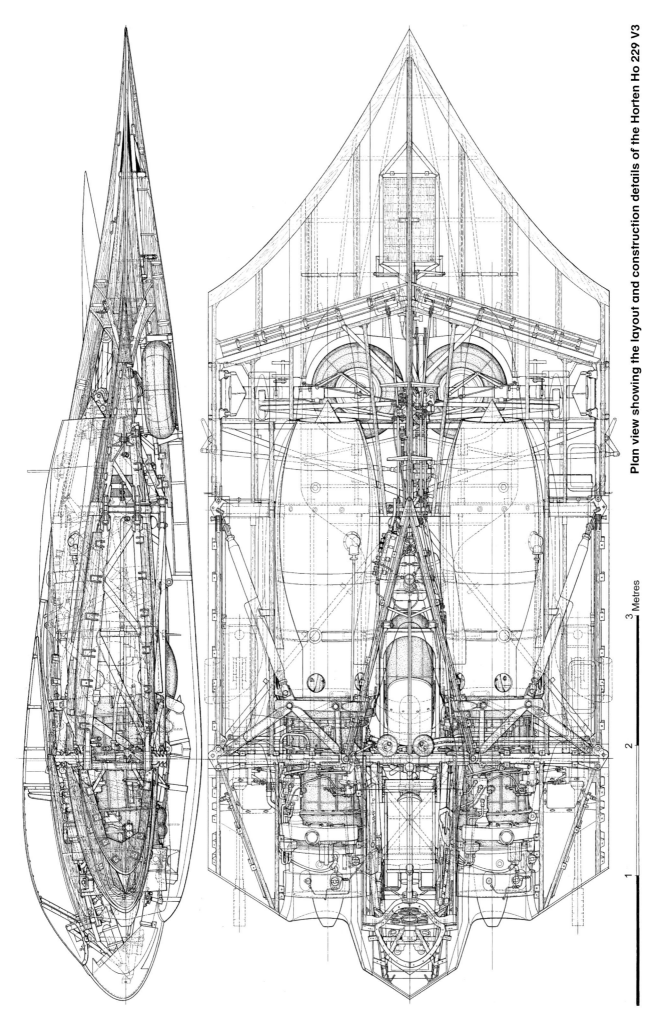

Plan view showing the layout and construction details of the Horten Ho 229 V3

3 Metres

2

1

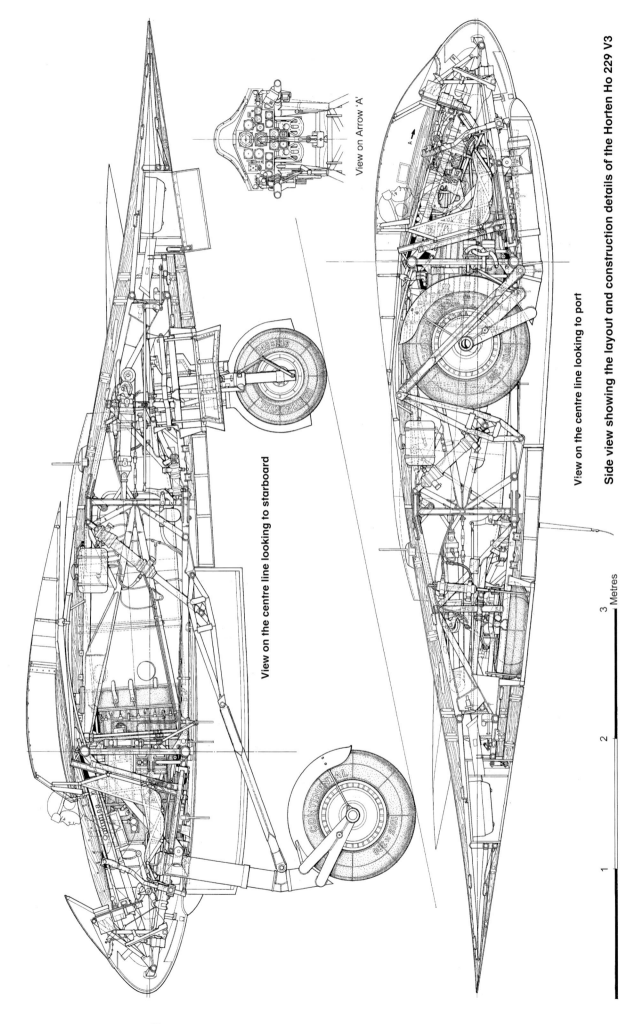

View on Arrow 'A'

View on the centre line looking to starboard

View on the centre line looking to port

Side view showing the layout and construction details of the Horten Ho 229 V3

Metres

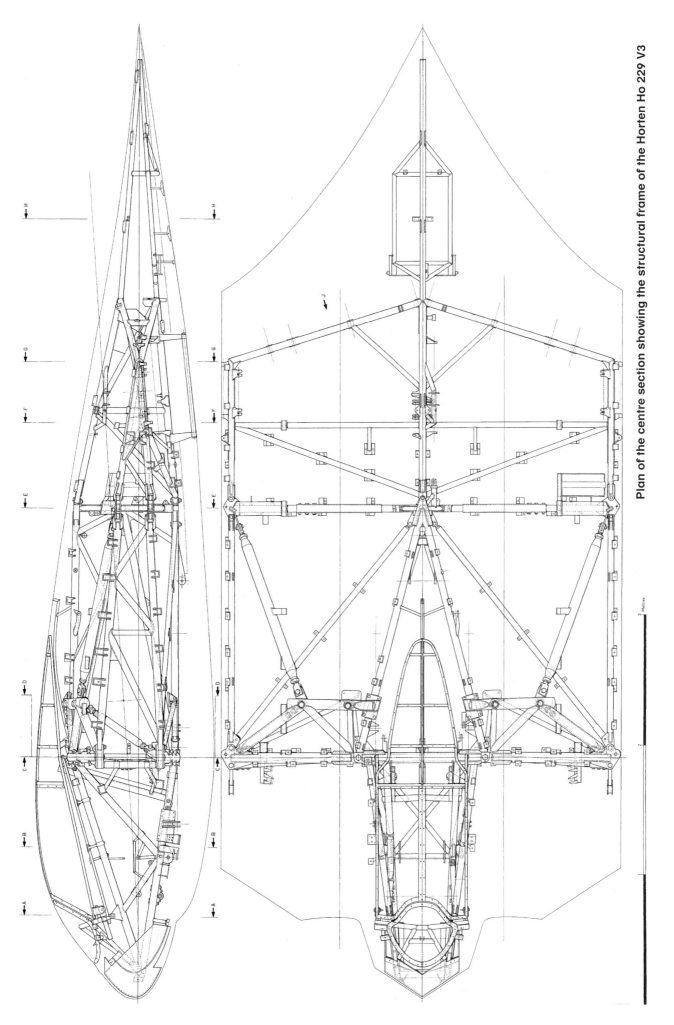

Plan of the centre section showing the structural frame of the Horten Ho 229 V3

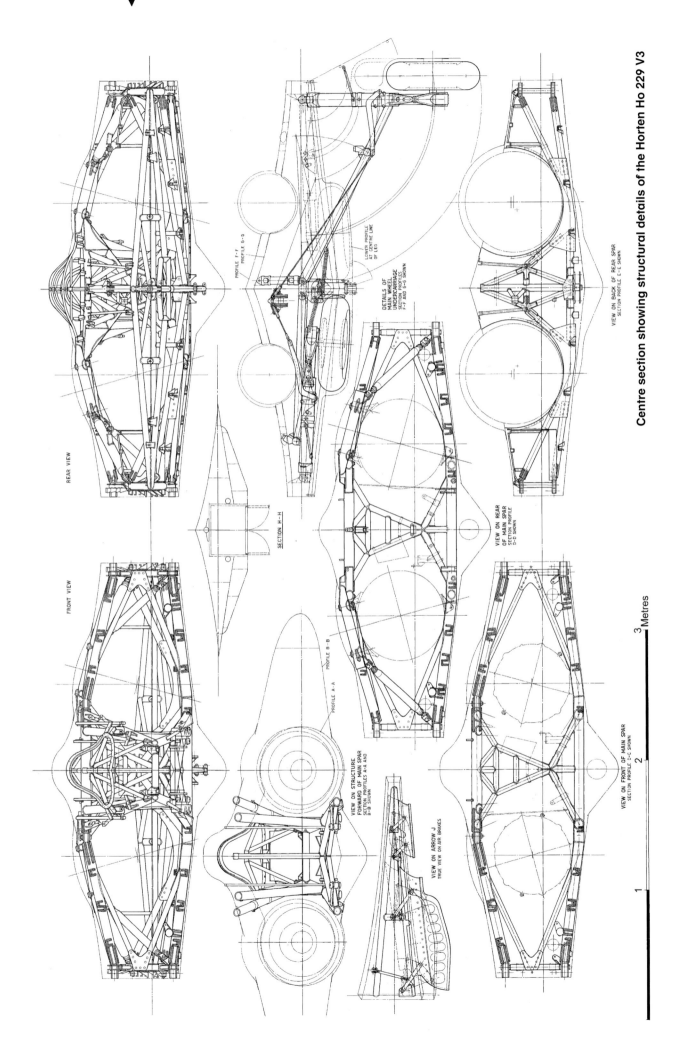

REAR VIEW

FRONT VIEW

PROFILE F-F
PROFILE G-G

LOWER PROFILE
AT CENTRE LINE
OF LEG

DETAILS OF
MAIN WHEEL
UNDERCARRIAGE
SECTION PROFILES
F-F AND G-G SHOWN

SECTION H-H

PROFILE B-B

PROFILE A-A

VIEW ON STRUCTURE
FORWARD OF MAIN SPAR
SECTION PROFILES A-A AND
B-B SHOWN

VIEW ON ARROW J
TRUE VIEW ON AIR BRAKES

VIEW ON REAR
OF MAIN SPAR
SECTION PROFILE
D-D SHOWN

VIEW ON FRONT OF MAIN SPAR
SECTION PROFILE C-C SHOWN

VIEW ON BACK OF REAR SPAR
SECTION PROFILE E-E SHOWN

Centre section showing structural details of the Horten Ho 229 V3

Metres

1   2   3

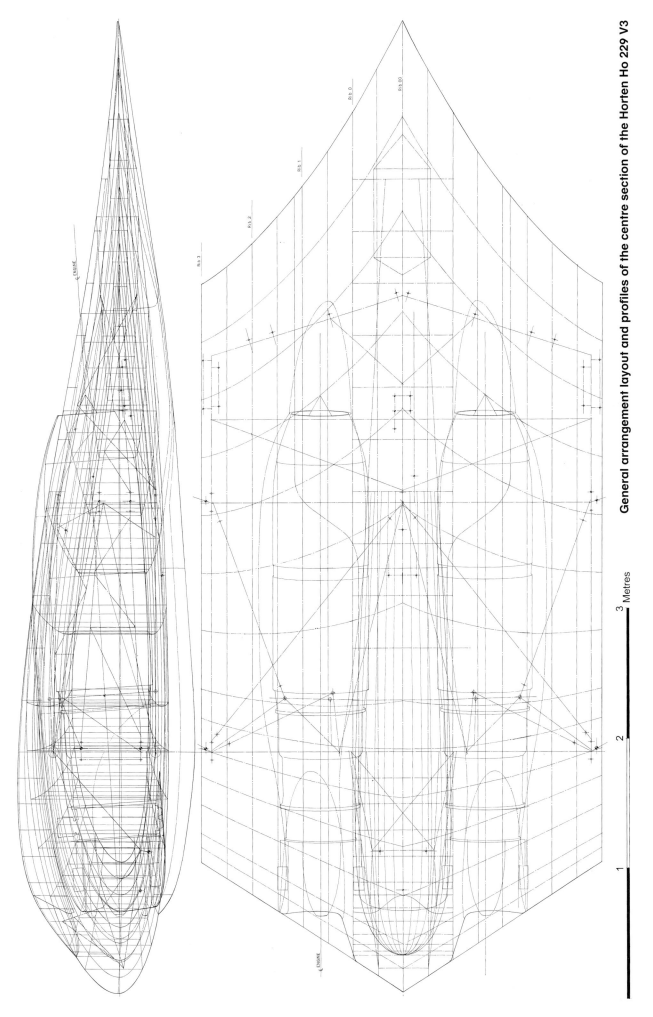

General arrangement layout and profiles of the centre section of the Horten Ho 229 V3

3 Metres

2

1

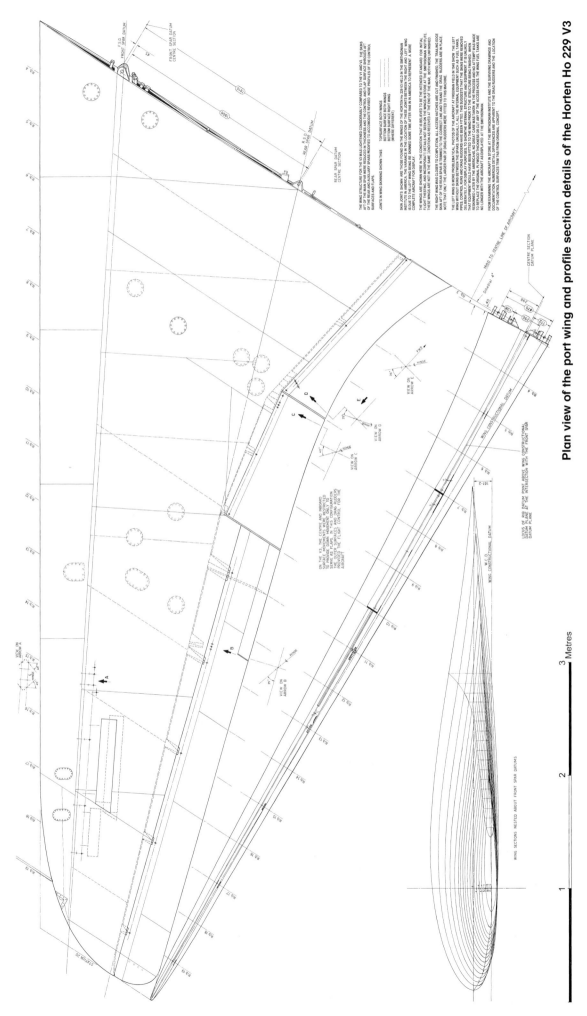

Plan view of the port wing and profile section details of the Horten Ho 229 V3

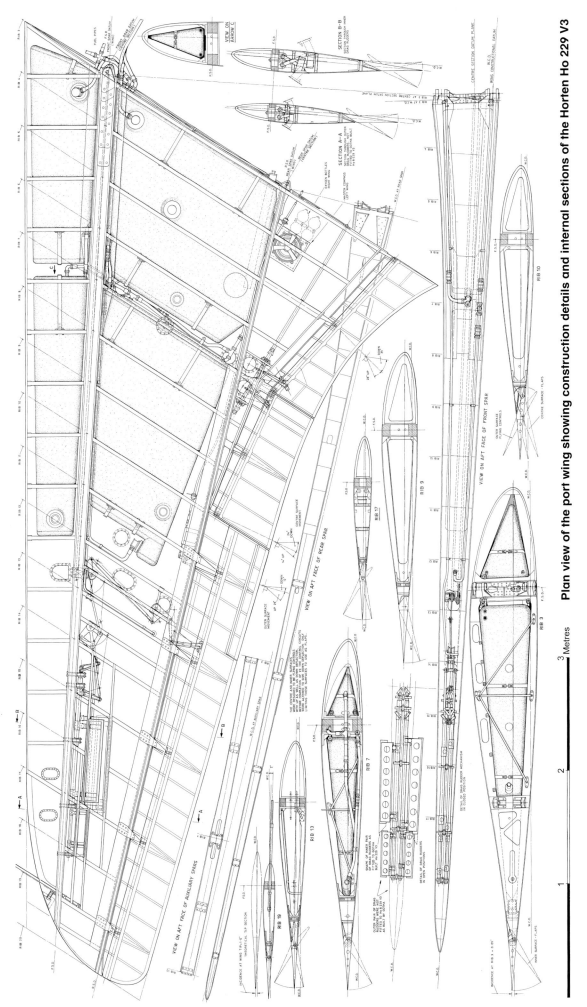

Plan view of the port wing showing construction details and internal sections of the Horten Ho 229 V3

Apart from the Ho 229 prototypes left at the Ortlepp GWF facility, another flying wing was reportedly found at Friedrichroda in a shed belonging to a local coal trader.[64] About half a kilometre from the shed, a GWF machine shop had been hidden in a railway tunnel, which also served as an air raid shelter. The flying wings were later taken away by the Americans.

On 6 May 1945 the H IX V1 glider was found at Leipzig-Brandis airfield by troops of the US 9th Armored Division slightly damaged and disassembled, although all other aircraft on the site had been destroyed. General McDonald, Director of the US Strategic Air Forces Intelligence in Europe, reported that: *"The Ho IX Glider Wing is believed to be of good technical value and the necessary arrangements have been made for removal to Merseburg"* – 20 km west of Leipzig where the US Air Technical Intelligence (ATI) had a collection site for valuable *Luftwaffe* hardware.[65]

The US Strategic Air Forces Intelligence in Europe (USSTAF A-2) had a great interest in the Hortens. On 9 May 1945 the brothers were flown in a Douglas C-47 transport aircraft to Britain for questioning at USSTAF (Rear) Intelligence Headquarters, along with their papers to be used during the interrogation. Soon the location of the design drawings of the 8-229 was disclosed. The drawings had been copied onto two reels of microfilm and buried somewhere in Friedrichroda before it was overrun by the US Army. On 12 May 1945 it was reported that two drums full of drawings were dug up by ATI personnel. They were taken away, together with *Herr* Eckhardt Kaufmann, a GWF supervisor for the construction and assembly of the 8-229, to an ATI Packing and Crating Centre

code-named 'GUNFIRE' in a village called Wolfgang (now part of Hanau) near Frankfurt. By that time one complete 8-229 (V3) and "parts of another" (V4) had already been transferred to GUNFIRE, and probably arrived there before May 1945.[66] The Americans hurried to secure their booty of advanced German technology before the eastern part of Germany, including the Gotha area, fell into the hands of the Soviet occupation forces.

Back in London, the Hortens were interviewed by Kenneth Wilkinson of the Royal Aircraft Establishment (RAE) during 19-21 May 1945. During these interviews the British learned of another H IX that had been hidden in a barn at Rodach near Coburg, and were given the details of the location. The remains of what was almost certainly the ill-fated V2 were later retrieved by American troops.[67]

Around the end of May 1945 the 9th AFSC was requested to crate the Horten "bat-wing aircraft" and prepare them for shipment to Wright Field. However it was then decided to leave the "additional parts" (V4) at the Packing and Crating Centre, where most probably they were later scrapped.[68] Meanwhile, by urgent request from the commander of the USAAF, General Henry 'Hap' Arnold, the Horten brothers were brought back to Germany to uncover the remaining hidden Horten aircraft and relating documents.[69]

On 7 June 1945 a team tasked with searching for the German gliders flew from Hendon in a C-47. Among the team members were C.W. Prower, chief designer of General Aircraft Ltd., sailplane manufacturer Fred Slingsby, Flt. Lt Narbeth and the great British sailplane authority, Chris Wills Sr.[70]

The remains of the H IX V1 at Kassel-Rothwesten.

Eric Brown (left), the British test pilot, seen here as a Lieutenant Commander at Crail in 1944, with P.G Lawrence who would later become the Chief Test Pilot for the Blackburn Aircraft Company. Brown, who had good contacts in pre-war Germany, first learned about the Horten brothers and their flying wings from Ernst Udet in 1936. In 1945 the H IV coded LA+AC (W.Nr. 25) was captured at Göttingen and transported to the RAE Farnborough. It was not until 13 May 1947 that Eric Brown flew the H IV for the first time. During the flight he found that the H IV had only marginal directional stability, sluggish lateral control but also light and effective longitudinal control which gave it good circling ability. His limited experience with the H IV did not convince him of the virtues bestowed on the aircraft by the Horten brothers, but he was positive about the prone-pilot position.

On 11 June 1945 the Horten-British team found several Horten sailplanes hidden at the Gut Tierstein farm. The H IIIf (W.Nr. 32), H IIIh (W.Nr. 31) and H IV (W.Nr. 26) gliders were recovered from the farm barns, all "…in perfect condition in trailers, with a full set of instruments."[71] The H IVb master drawings were also found in a small workshop.

At the same time, an ATI branch at Roth near Nürnberg was requested to recover an H VI glider stored inside a mill near Bad Hersfeld. They found the H VI V2 in good condition but missing all instruments. Again, no drawings were found at the site, as these had been taken away by a courier the day before the place was overrun by Allied forces. Otherwise, the facility had been surrendered intact in accordance with the Hortens' order,[72] and the glider complete with its trailer went for shipment to the US. The location of the hidden drawings was not kept secret for long, as they were soon recovered by the British from a salt mine in Bad Salzdetfurth 50 km north of Göttingen.[73]

In the middle of June 1945 all the Horten gliders were still considered a "high priority target" and were earmarked for shipment to the USA under Operation 'Seahorse' which was intended to preserve valuable German aircraft.[74] Only a week later the interest suddenly waned and it was decided that the Horten gliders were of no intelligence interest. As such, they were scheduled for shipment to the RAE in Farnborough.[75] At this point the H IX V1 prototype was reported as being prepared for shipment to Wright Field, together with the V3,[76] but this was later abandoned and burned at Kassel-Rothwesten airfield. Before the British group returned home around 20-22 June 1945, they witnessed the V3 being towed down the autobahn in the direction of Kassel, where it was probably originally planned to join the V1 for their 'Seahorse' ride to America. On 26 June, a Ho 229 (obviously the V3) was dispatched by train to the port of Cherbourg,[77] where it was loaded aboard a Liberty Ship SS *Richard J. Gatling* and thence shipped to the USA on 12 July 1945.[78]

Even before the Ho 229 V3 reached America around 1 August 1945, her older sister machine had already landed in England. The H IX V2 remains were flown in July 1945 from Binders airfield near Erfurt to the RAE Farnborough, squeezed into a cargo hold of a captured Arado Ar 232. The aircraft was loaned from General McDonald by the renowned British test pilot, Captain Eric Brown. It was considered for employment as an experimental aircraft to study the flying wing concept within a transonic research project initiated at the RAE. Here the possibility of re-engining the aircraft with Rolls Royce Avon turbo jets was discussed, since the British test pilots refused to fly the Ho 229 with 'unreliable' Jumos. In fact, several Jumo 004B-powered Ar 234s and Me 262s were being tested successfully at the same time in Farnborough. The unwillingness of the RAE pilots to take the Ho 229's controls is quite understandable taking into account some of the design features of this experimental aircraft. In particular, there were no walls to separate the cockpit from the engines and the nose undercarriage well (the same as on the second prototype) and no firewalls to isolate the engine compressor sections from the fuel tanks. So, the Ho 229 pilot had to take off while being sandwiched between the two roaring turbojets, with an appreciable draught coming from the open undercarriage doors, with his hips close to the engine oil tanks and his body close to the compressor. Such a hostile environment left little chance of survival in the case of a very probable engine failure.

The H IV sailplane on display in the 'A' Hangar at Farnborough, England.

It was soon established that, because of its large cross-section, the Rolls-Royce centrifugal engine could not be installed in the Ho 229 without considerable modification of the airframe.[79] To close the matter, it was decided that even the re-engined Ho 229 would lack the necessary performance. The project was abandoned in favour of an idea for a prone position, Rolls-Royce Avon powered aircraft, a proposal that was outlined in Tech Note Aero 1928 by two German aero-dynamicists, M. Winter and H.Multhopp.[80]

Next month the Horten brothers were again interrogated by a British team, this time one initiated by the Tailless Advisory Committee. The team comprising Wilkinson, Prower, Watson, Lee, Robert Kronfeld and Geoffrey Hill, flew from the RAE to Braunschweig-Volkenrode on 17 September 1945. Three days later the team arrived at the AVA in Göttingen and spent until 2 October 1945 interrogating the Hortens for several hours a day with Kronfeld translating.[81] This "...included a visit to a local airfield to see some of the Horten machines... the strangest was a flying 'tube' fuselage with swept-back wings intended to be used as a wind tunnel" (H VIII). On the return flight from Göttingen the team picked up the H IV W.Nr. 25 LA-AC; this was impressed into RAF service as VP543. It was first flown at Farnborough on 11 October 1945 and then displayed in the 'A' Hangar during the October/November German Aircraft Exhibition. The H IV/VP543 was tested at the RAE until 1950, usually towed by a captured Fieseler Fi 156 (AM 101/VP546).

At the same exhibition in Farnborough's 'A' Hangar, a collection of fragments of what had previously been the H IX V2 was displayed. The engineless remnants showed up exactly as they ended up in Oranienburg, with one wing and the cockpit being virtually demolished. According to Eric Brown's recollections, the H IX was sent to the USA in the autumn of 1945 or in 1946;[82] the only

The Horten (Gotha) 8-229 V3 at Freeman Field, Indiana, USA. The X-shaped detail in the nose-wheel strut is not a part of the undercarriage design. It is possible that this was a brace to keep the undercarriage from a possible collapse. Note the poor fit of the lower skin panels. The metallic panels seem to have been partially primed. The plywood skin was not painted. Reimar Horten recalled in his conversation with Reinhold Stadler that no specific colour schemes were pursued on the H IX; instead, any available paint was used.

document that indirectly confirms this statement also mentions the shipment of a "Horten 8". It is not known if this information is correct and nothing is known about the fate of these remains.[83]

Almost concurrent with the Farnborough exhibition, on the opposite side of the Atlantic, two other Horten all-wing aircraft were being displayed

Unloading of the Ho 229 V3 from a railroad car at Freeman Field, Indiana, 1945. (Photo by Howard Furst).

at Freeman Field air base near Seymour, Indiana. The Ho 229 V3 had been assigned the enemy equipment number 'FE-490' by the Americans, but this changed early in 1946 to 'T2-490' (T-2 was the organisation designator for USAAF Air Technical Intelligence). There was a plan to test-fly the aircraft, calling for as much as 15,000 man-hours to complete the airframe. This plan was later rejected due to the post-war military budget reductions and the complexity of the task. By late January 1946 it was considered *"...that reconstruction is not feasible and is impossible without a re-design of the basic aircraft."* Besides the largely complete centre section, only one (starboard) incomplete wing panel of the Ho 229 V3 was available at Freeman Field, the wing missing the lower skin behind the main spar and brake rudders.[84]

Nevertheless, both wing panels were later gathered and covered with a low-grade plywood of reduced thickness; the aircraft was given false *'Luftwaffe'* camouflage and off-register markings. Following deactivation of the Freeman Field air base in the summer of 1946, the Ho 229 V3 was transferred to No.903 Special Depot at Park Ridge, Illinois. There, in the halls of the former Douglas factory located at the Orchard airfield (now O'Hare Chicago International Airport), more than 80 Second World War aircraft had been gathered by order of USAF commander General Arnold for a planned Air Force Technical Museum. In September 1947 this collection went into the possession of the National Air Museum (NAM), a division of the Smithsonian Institution established in 1946 (becoming the National Air & Space Museum, NASM in 1966). After the outbreak of the Korean War, General Arnold's collection was nearly bulldozed when the

order came to vacate the factory it occupied for a planned deployment of an additional C-119 assembly line. Owing to the efforts of the Museum's curator, Paul E. Garber, the collection was moved in 1952 to a woodland near Silver Hill, Maryland. Due to limited hangar space being available, most of the large size artefacts such as the Ho 229 V3 had to be stored outdoors, exposed to the elements for more than 10 years.

The other Horten aircraft seen at the 1945 Freeman Field display was the H II L (W.Nr. 6, D-10-125, T2-7), reportedly recovered at Kempten some 90 km south-west of Munich.[85]

The Ho 229 V3 in a hangar at Freeman Field, Indiana. In the background can be seen a starboard wing panel without the lower skin and journalists visiting the base during an 'open house' event.

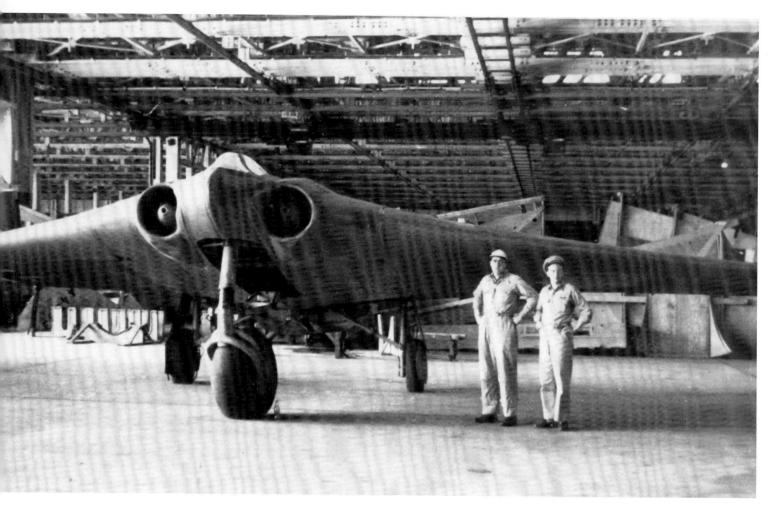

It has been universally accepted until now that the outer wings of the Ho 229 V3 had never been attached to its centre section. This photograph is published for the first time here by courtesy of Richard Kik Jr. and depicts the Horten Ho 229 assembled with its wings at the Douglas factory in Chicago for display purposes.

Beside the H VI V2 (W.Nr. 34, LA-AL, T2-5040), two other Horten gliders, the H IIIf (W.Nr. 32, T2-5042) and the H IIIh (W.Nr. 31, LA-AI, T2-5039), were shipped to the USA by 1946. After two years of languishing at Freeman Field they were loaned to Northrop on 22 October 1947. The original intention was to test-fly the two H IIIs, but they arrived so badly damaged that their repair was considered impractical. The almost airworthy H VI was not flown either, due to the danger of flutter. The following year all three aircraft were returned to Park Ridge.

The RAE's H IV (W.Nr. 25 LA-AC) was also shipped to the USA after repair in 1950, receiving US registration N79289. The following year Rudolf Opitz flew it in two soaring contests, winning the first. Rudi Opitz was a former Messerschmitt test pilot who had tested the Me 163 and also participated in the Eben-Emael air assault operation with Ziller and Scheidhauer. Later, the N79289 found its way to Mississippi State University where it was tested in 1959. Having already accumulated some 1,000 flying hours by 1945, this glider was probably the most extensively flown Horten-built aircraft. Currently it is on display at the Planes of Fame Museum in Chino, California.

The H IV W.Nr. 26 from the Gut Tierstein farm remained in Germany at the disposal of a glider club of the British forces (BAFO), who wanted to have it repaired and therefore ordered a new set of wings to replace the missing originals. As there were no skilled craftsmen around to re-manufacture the wings along the original design, Reimar Horten designed the simplified all-wooden outer wings without the brake rudders. Thus the first 'single control' Horten aircraft was built. Unfortunately, during the first flight by Heinz Scheidhauer the adverse yaw was so strong that the glider was considered dangerous and consequently was tried only once by another pilot.[86] According to other sources, the left wing of W.Nr. 26 was damaged on landing in the early 1950s and was never flown again. Over the years the centre section was lost and just the two outer wings remained. By 1999 the H IV W.Nr. 26 had been restored with a newly-built centre section and put on display at the Flugwerft Schleißheim of the Deutsches Museum near Munich. Part of the wing of the ill-fated H IVb W.Nr. 40 is also stored at this location.

The other surviving Horten gliders were in the NAM/NASM possession since 1949, and in 1993 were transferred to the *Museum für Verkehr und Technik* (MVT, now Deutsches Technik Museum) in Berlin. Following completion of the restoration in the spring of 2004, the H IIIf and the H VI V2 have been placed on display at the NASM Steven F. Udvar-Hazy Center at Dulles airport in Washington DC, while the H IIL and the H IIIh remain in Germany as a compensation for the original development work. The H IIL is on display at DTM in Berlin.

The H VI V2, now on display at the NASM Steven F Udvar-Hazy Center at Dulles Airport in Washington DC.

The windscreen and canopy of
the Ho 229 V3 in its current state
at time of writing at the
Paul E. Garber restoration
facility of the NASM at Silver Hill
in Maryland, USA.

A photograph showing the
current status of the Ho 229 V3's
cockpit. Some of the instruments
have been removed for other
restoration projects.

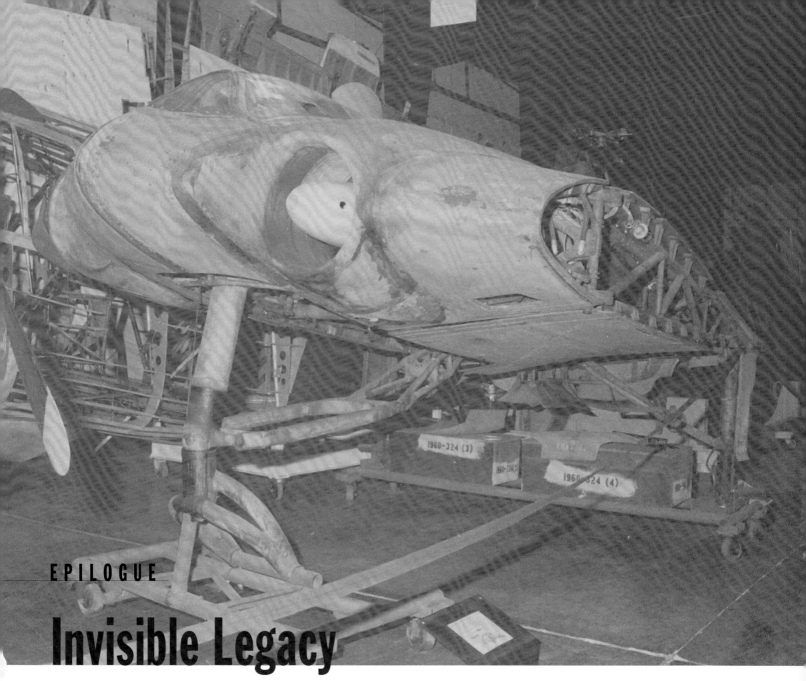

EPILOGUE

Invisible Legacy

WHILE the military career of the Horten aircraft from 'Operation *Seelöwe*' through to 'Operation Seahorse' was limited mainly to painting *Balkenkreuze* on their wings, the Hortens' ultimate contribution to aeronautics is still to be fully comprehended. Just why they never succeeded in making their *Nurflügel* ideas a real success is perhaps a double-sided issue. On the one hand, the flying wing concept was probably years ahead of its time and only now are technology and aerodynamic science able to overcome its inherent limitations. This is probably confirmed by the results of the parallel all-wing endeavour by John K. Northrop in the United States. This fared far better in much better conditions but did not achieve a break-through either.

On the other side, Reimar's 'all-wing-or-nothing' isolationism left the Hortens outside the industry mainstream during the war and later. The opportunity to further their work was granted by the British as soon as the interrogations were over, despite Reimar's unwillingness at first to cooperate without a contract. Under British control the H VIII project was being developed into a 70-100 ton transport until at least 1946. That year Reimar

obtained his PhD degree in mathematics. He thought that if he had earned his PhD already in 1940 he would, in the eyes of the aviation community, "not have been a boy building sailplanes but a respected colleague…"

In 1947 Reimar tried to find work in England, France or the USA; his attempt to join Northrop through the 'Paperclip' channels failed for unknown reasons, as did the possible employment with de Havilland. A natural partner for the Hortens could have been the British firm of Armstrong-Whitworth, which flew a scaled-down flying wing glider prototype in 1945, followed by the full-size twin-jet AW-52 in 1947. The same year the Vulcan near-flying-wing bomber was initiated at AVRO, also preceded by a scaled-down prototype. Yet, the public sentiments in Britain were against the employment of defeated Germans. Talks were in progress with Richard Fairey, whose son flew the H IV at Cologne, but the Fairey workers refused to work with a German.

During the war Reimar did not refrain from visiting the concentration camps in Sachsenhausen and Nordhausen – to claim later that the situation there, as pictured by the Allied media, "…was a thing of propaganda".[87] Forced labour was used at the Horten works. By the end of the war Walter was promoted to *Major*; and Reimar to *Hauptmann* (Captain) and awarded the *Kriegsverdienstkreuz mit Schwerten, Erste Klasse.*

Since his attempts to join the former enemy had failed, Reimar disappointed and embittered, turned his attention to other countries with aviation ambitions. Back in 1945 he had discussed with Kurt Tank an offer to work in China; two years later Tank invited Reimar to Argentina to help design the *Pulqui II* jet fighter. This work was not a success, but after Tank's team left for India, Reimar remained in Argentina for the rest of his life. Here at the periphery of aviation life, and with the help of his old comrades Heinz Scheidhauer and Karl Nickel, he produced a number of interesting projects. The supersonic dream was given a try again and the H VIII was finally flown in the form of the IAe.38 tailless transport, finalising the story of the Horten aircraft in 1960.

By the late 1970s the brothers were still interested in carrying on their work and hoped to obtain support from a US sponsor or manufacturer for the development of an ultra high-performance sailplane. Reimar was convinced that this could be done with contemporary materials and technologies. He was also looking for a bright and interested student of aerodynamics to come to his family ranch *Athos Pampa* in Córdoba to inherit his principles and ideas.

The flying wing was neither the Hortens' invention nor their monopoly; what Reimar considered his exclusive brainchild was the bell-shaped lift distribution theory. Since this magic formula had never made the Hortens' hoped-for fortune, Reimar published it in 1981 in *Soaring* magazine, and later in the autobiographic book *Nurflügel*. To Reimar's disappointment, he found that only a few readers understood his theory.

Despite the statements made by Dr. Reimar Horten, it appears that there are no documents available to confirm the introduction of the BSLD to any of the Horten aircraft until at least the war's end. The existing Horten drawings show that at least the H IIIb, H XII and H IX had a linear wing twist not matching the BSLD. Karl Nickel, who made the majority of the lift-distribution and stress calculations for the Horten designs, is quite certain that not one of them possessed the genuine BSLD. He states that he never heard about this theory from Reimar Horten before they parted in 1955 and that Walter could not confirm that he knew of the BSLD either.

Karl Nickel also points out that no Horten aircraft had the claimed proverse (or at least neutral) yawing moment. Instead, most of them had significant adverse yaw. This is why they were equipped with the drag rudders for directional control and the 'exaggerated' Frise-nose elevons providing some compensating drag on the up-going elevon.

One possible explanation for Reimar's claims was his limited experience with all-wing aircraft that obviously did not extend beyond the early H II flights. This aircraft was trimmed extremely nose-heavy for Reimar, which was, according to Nickel, sufficient by itself for the aircraft to have a pro-verse yaw moment. And Reimar was sufficiently stubborn not to hear the other pilots' reports about the adverse yaw on most of the Horten types.

The reason for the retrospective way in which Reimar attributed the BSLD to his designs was probably a form of wishful thinking which made him sometimes mix up his thoughts and desires with reality – a desire for recognition that he undoubtedly deserved but never received during his lifetime…

Reimar Horten passed away on 14 August 1993. Two days after his death he was posthumously awarded the Gold Medal of the Royal Aeronautical Society for his contribution to aeronautical science. He was only the second German to receive this award.

Walter Horten passed away on 9 December 1998. He made a significant contribution to the creation of the post-war German *Bundesluftwaffe.*

"Studies made in Great Britain and the United States, with flying wings and 'Delta' wing aircraft for high speed, indicate that the advantages of this kind of construction are being recognized there. So, the investigations made in Germany, from the point of view of aeronautic science, show that they were not in vain."

Reimar Horten, 1952

In the late 1970s and early 1980s, information began to appear in the mass-media regarding the development in the United States of technologies for a 'low observable' combat aircraft, better known as 'Stealth' technology. Research was being conducted to find materials and configurations with which to reduce the radar and infra-red visibility of aircraft. The flying wing layout was found to have the smallest possible vertical plane areas and hence the least radar-reflecting surface, while its simple shape precluded the deflection of the incoming electromagnetic waves in the direction of the signal source, i.e. the searching radar.

Originating from this research the 'Stealth' warplanes such as the Northrop B-2A and the projected McDonnell Douglas A-12 appeared to have design features strikingly reminiscent of the Horten Ho 229. No wonder that the astounding idea of 'Nazi Stealth' arose and became almost universally accepted by the media. Could it be true that the technology which we consider to be one of the latest developments in aerial warfare has, in fact, its roots in the Third Reich? Let us look again at the time of the H IX inception.

Evidently the problem of avoiding radar detection came into being the moment the first operational radar was fielded. Already during the Battle of Britain radar had greatly enhanced the effectiveness of the British air defence. As early as April 1942 the RLM's Director of Air Armament, Erhard Milch, offered a prize for finding a way of

The Ho 229 V3: 1-metal wingtip fairing; 2-pitot tube; 3-elevon; 4-elevon trim tab; 5-drag rudder spring compensating mechanism; 6-drag rudder; 7-drag rudder control linkage; 8-elevon hinges; 9-elevon linkage; 10-fuel tank; 11-electric fuel pump; 12-inner struts; 13-fuel tank support straps; 14-outer flap; 15-inner flap; 16-main spar; 17-rear spar; 18-auxiliary spar; 19-nose rib: 20-rib: 21-main spar root strengthening; 22-main spar root attachment fittings; 23-rear spar attachment fittings; 24-flap actuator rod; 25-rear spar strengthening; 26-flap skew hinge control link; 27-nose centre section skin; 28-skin seam metal reinforcing stripe; 29-oil tank filler hatch; 30-Riedel starter motor fuel filler hatch; 31-start fuel for Jumo 004 filler hatch; 32-air intake; 33-accessory drive gear; 34-engine bearing frame; 35-radio compartment hatch; 36-engine bearing case; 37-engine firewall; 38-exhaust cone drive gear; 39-master compass access hatch; 40-fairing for u/c up sensor in up position; 41-exhaust duct; 42-exhaust steel panel; 43-bleed air exit louvres; 44-spoiler control bell-crank access hatch; 45-brake chute compartment; 46-spoiler control levers; 47-spoiler control rod; 48-brake chute reinforced attachment point; 49-wheel-mounted main u/c door section; 50-hinged main u/c door section; 51-main u/c strut; 52-main u/c pull cable; 53-main u/c inner door section; 54-main u/c deploying spring; 55-main u/c inner door and locking hydraulic actuator; 56-main u/c hydraulic retraction jack; 57-main u/c cable drive pulleys; 58-flap hydraulic actuator; 59-flap actuator linkage; 60-hydraulic system distribution board; 61-hydraulic fluid reservoir; 62-nose u/c hydraulic retraction jack; 63-nose u/c locking mechanism bracket; 64-nose u/c strut; 65-nose u/c door; 66-nose u/c door operating mechanism; 67-upper engine attachment points; 68-lower engine attachment point; 69-framework engine bearing strengthening; 70-engine bearing strut; 71-fuel pipeline; 72-centre section root rib; 73-skin fixing fitting; 74-fuel filler caps; 75-rear canopy rail; 76- canopy metal skin section; 77-bell-cranks of spoiler and brake chute doors linkages; 78-ejection seat; 79-ejection seat rails; 80-control linkage; 81-canopy jettison spring; 82-ballast; 83-nose u/c door fairing; 84-control column linkage; 85-rudder pedals linkage; 86-rudder pedals levers; 87-nose oleo leg; 88-castoring nosewheel welded steel tube fork; 89-direction finder antenna.

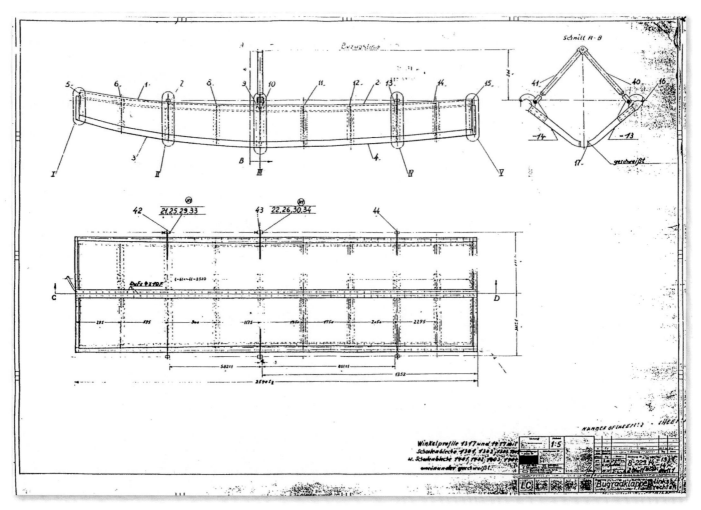

Surviving drawings of the Ho 229 V3 made a reliable reconstruction possible of the missing undercarriage doors and fairing.

deceiving enemy radar.[88] While airborne electronic warfare was in the event pioneered by the British 'Window' passive jamming, it was the German Navy which introduced the means of permanent radar-protection of moving vehicles. By 1944 the *Kriegsmarine* had developed and tested radar-absorbing materials which were applied to the parts of submarines exposed above water in order to prevent their detection by ASV radar, which was a naval version of the H2S airborne radar. The simplest material was a carbon-impregnated rubber coating, named *'Schornsteinfeger'* ('chimney sweeper'), an allusion to the substance used.

Although the Ho 229 has been immediately identified as "stealthy" due to the characteristics of its overall configuration, neither of the Horten brothers ever claimed their aircraft had been designed with consideration to the way it *deflects* radar waves. In fact, the unique shape of the Ho 229 had evolved from the ten-year long *aerodynamic* research by the Hortens. What Reimar *did* claim as far back as 1950, was that the wooden construction of the Ho 229 would *reflect* very little of the incoming electromagnetic waves, thus making the aircraft *"...barely visible on the radar".*[89]

Here it should be noted that despite a widespread belief, the wooden construction of an aircraft does not necessarily reduce its radar visibility. Known is the fact that the all-wooden de Havilland Mosquito was in no way 'invisible'. It is true that wood is a predominantly

radio-transparent material, reflecting and dissipating only a small fraction of radiation. But, with the skin transparent to the radar rays, the inner structures such as the engines or the tubular frame of the Ho 229 would reflect the incoming radiation none the less.

It appears that the radar-absorption properties of carbon had not been known to Reimar before the late 1970s, when materials working on similar principles were created in the USA. Perhaps this new information led Reimar to assert in his "visionary" manner that the charcoal present inside the *Formholz* skin of the Ho 229 *"...would diffuse radar beams, and make the aircraft 'invisible' to radar."*[90] Although the charcoal, being a form of carbon, could in fact dissipate electromagnetic emissions in a limited range of wavelengths, this substance had actually been utilised as a porous filler to lighten the composite formed parts. Another variation of the carbon theme by Reimar dealt with a mix of coal dust and glue that *"...camouflaged 90 % of the radar cross-section of the Ho 229"* and had to be applied also to the H XVIII.[91]

While no wartime document is known to confirm any 'stealth' activities within the *Luftwaffe,* the Horten 229 can in any event be considered a precursor to the latest flying wing, the blended-wing-body and related developments, both military and civil – stealth or not. Thus, seventy years on, the Hortens' vision is still at the forefront of aeronautical progress.

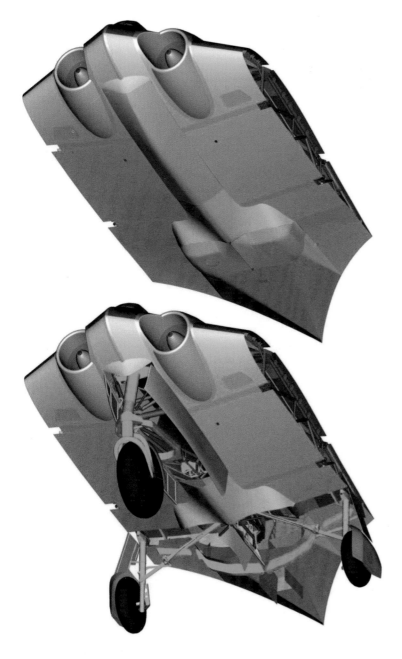

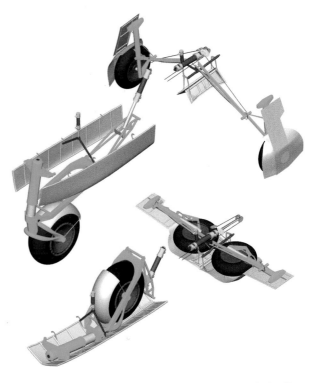

Both the 8-229 main undercarriage legs retracted by a single hydraulic jack through cable drive pulleys. The pull cable free-end attached to a strut-breaker lever. Undercarriage deployment was effected by means of a spring. The main undercarriage was blocked in the up position by the hydraulically-activated and locked inner doors. The nose undercarriage leg was blocked by a locking mechanism.

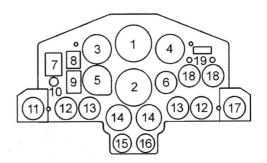

The Ho 229 V3 cockpit: 1-turn and bank indicator; 2-repeater compass; 3-vertical speed indicator; 4-airspeed indicator; 5-altimeter; 6-AFN2 direction finder indicator; 7-undercarriage position indicators: upper row – nose gear down (red) / up, lower – main gears, left /right; 8- ignition breakers left/right engine; 9-flaps position indicators, top to bottom: landing, take-off, up; 10-emergency circuit breaker; 11-hydraulic system pressure gauge; 12-oil pressure left/right engines; 13-exhaust temperature left/right engines; 14-rpm left/right engines; 15-oxygen pressure; 16-oxygen indicator; 17-ambient temperature gauge; 18-fuel gauges; 19-low fuel warning; 20-fuel pressure gauge; 21-fuel tanks switches; 22-brake chute doors opening lever (reconstruction); 23-spoiler release lever; 24-flaps and undercarriage retraction levers; 25-throttles; 26-canopy rail; 27-canopy fixing stub; 28-canopy emergency jettison handle; 29-ejection seat; 30-control column; 31-control column variable length fixing handle; 32-rudder pedals; 33-hydraulic toe brakes; 34-ejection seat lever; 35-communication board; 36-circuit breakers board; 37-engine front casing; 38-oil tank/cooler; 39- oil tank/cooler filler cap; 40- annular tank for starting fuel.

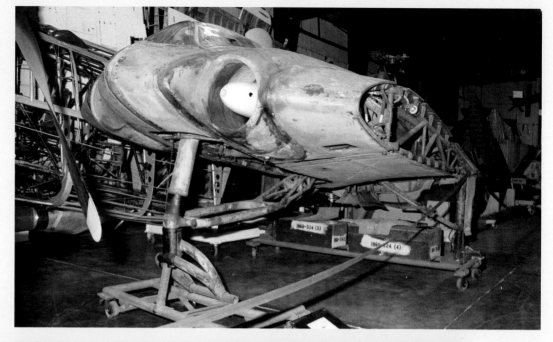

The sole surviving Ho 229, the V3, in storage in a hangar at the Paul E.Garber restoration facility of the Smithsonian National Air and Space Museum at Silver Hill, Maryland, USA. A 'walk-around' photo-sequence by courtesy of Geoff Steele and Russell Lee.

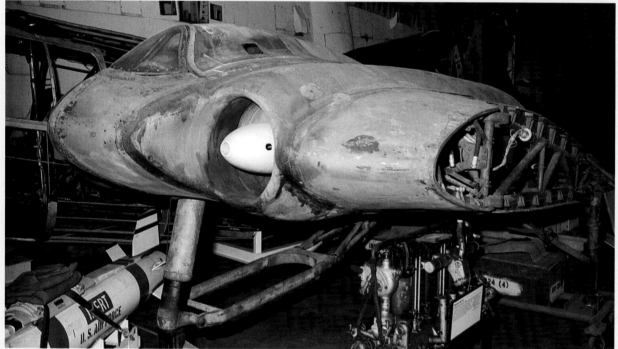

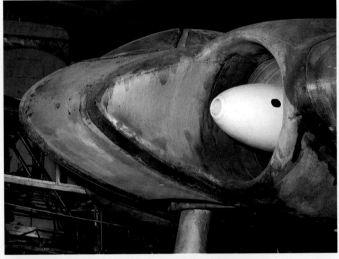

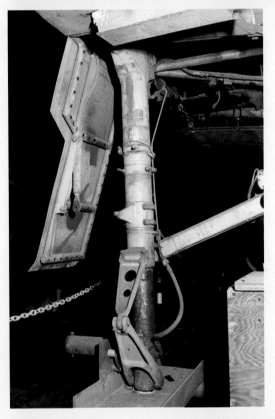

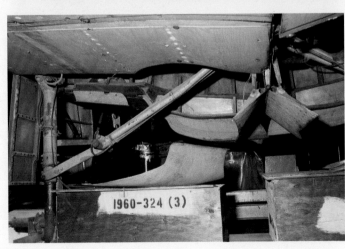

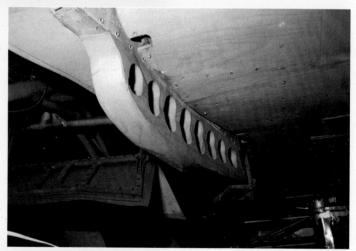

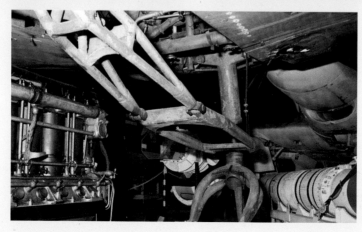

Comparison Weight Table (in Kg) Ho 229 vs. Go P-60a/Me 262A-2a/Ar 234B-2

	Ho 229 V6	Go P-60a	Me 262A-2a	Ar 234B-2
Centresection	1110	915		
Outer wings w/o tanks	1400	900		
Landing gear	345	525		
Powerplant	1735	1570		
Armour	400	290		
Pressure cabin	-	120		
Cannon 4x 30 mm MK 108	240	240		
Cannon auxiliary equipment	120	120		
Other equipment	220	180		
Empty weight	5570	4860	4100	5200
Crew	100	200	100	100
Landing weight	5670	5060	4200	5300
Ammunition	215	390	215	-
Weight w/o fuel	5885	5450	4415	5300
Fuel	2000	2000	2220	3117
Take-off weight	7885	7450	6635	8417

Performance Chart

	Empty weight, kg	Fuel capacity	Take-off weight with 500kg bombload	Maximum speed w/o external attachments, km/h at altitude	Combat range, km / at cruise speed, km/h, with 500 kg bombload	Combat range, km / at cruise speed, km/h, with 1000 kg bombload	Take-off distance w/o external attachments, m	Landing distance, m	Landing speed, km/h
Messerschmitt Me 262A-2a	4100	2565	7135	875/6000	? / 800	~850/~700	~1100	~1100	175
Horten/Gotha Ho 229 V6	5570	3000	8385	875/4000	1400/~780	~1200/~700	1100	?	157
Arado Ar 234B-2	5200	3750	8917	740/6000	1550/ 692	~1300/ 600	1600-1800	1330 (635 with brake chute)	146

Horten Specification Chart

	Wingspan (metres)	Height (metres)	Length (metres)	Wing area - m²	Leading edge sweepback (degrees)	1/4 chord sweepback (degrees)	Taper ratio	Aspect ratio	Thickness ratio at center section %	Wing root thickness %	Wing tip thickness %	Total washout %	Dihedral (degrees)
H I	12.4	1.50	3.1	21.0	23.0	9.5	5.7	7.3	25.0	20.0	10.0	7.0	3.0
H II	16.5	1.65	5.0	32.0	29.5	26.0	8.4	8.5	20.0	20.0	10.0	8.0	3.0
H IIm	16.5	1.65	5.0	32.0	29.5	26.0	8.4	8.5	20.0	20.0	10.0	8.0	3.0
H IIL	16.5	1.65	5.0	32.0	29.5	26.0	8.4	8.5	20.0	20.0	10.0	8.0	3.0
H III a/c	20.4	1.65	5.0	36.0	24.3	23.0	10.0	11.6	20.0	20.0	10.0		3.0
H IIIb	20.5	1.65	5.0	37.5	24.3	23.0	8.0	11.1	20.0	20.0	10.0		3.0
H IIId	20.5	1.65	5.0	37.5	24.3	23.0	8.0	11.1	20.0	20.0	10.0		3.0
H IIIe	20.5	1.65	5.0	37.5	24.3	23.0	8.0	11.1	20.0	20.0	10.0		3.0
H IIIf	20.5		5.0	37.5	24.3	23.0	8.0	11.1	20.0	20.0	10.0		3.0
H IIIg/h	20.5	1.65	5.0	37.5	24.3	23.0	8.0	11.1	20.0	20.0	10.0		3.0
H IVa	20.3	2.0	3.65	18.9	20	17.0	6.0	21.8	27.0	16.0	8.0	7.1	5.0
H IVb	20.3	2.0	3.65	18.9		18.0	6.0	21.8	27.0	15.5	10.0	5.6	5.0
H Va	14.0		5.4	34.0	25.5/40	32.0	6.4	5.45		18.0	8.0	5.0	3.0
H Vb	16.0	2.1	6.75	38.0	25.5/36	32.0	6.4	6.75		16.0	8.0	5.0	3.0
H Vc	16.0	2.1	6.75	38.0	25.5/36	32.0	6.4	6.75		16.0	8.0	5.0	3.0
H VI	24.2			17.8	16.7	15.0	7.0	32.4		16.0	8.0	6.2	5.0
H VII	16.0	2.5	7.5	44.0	40	34.0	8.0	5.8	17.0	16.0	8.0	5.0	2.5
H VIII	40.0	3.85	16.5	146.0	33.7	27.0	8.1	11.0	18.0	18.0	8.0	7.0	3.0
H IX V1	16.0	2.4	6.5	46.0	32.0	28.0*	7.5	5.6	15.0	13.8	8.0	1.0	4.0*
H IX V2	16.8	2.7	7.47	51.8	32.0	28.0*	7.8	5.35	15.5	13.8	8.0	1.05	4.0*
H IX V3	16.8	2.9	7.47	51.8	32.0	28.0*	7.8	5.35	15.5	13.8	8.0	1.05	4.0*
H X (FJ)	14.0	2.3	7.2										
H XII	15.0	1.65	5.0	38.5	29		6.0	6.7		13.0			
H XIIIa	12.0	1.5	11.0	36.0	60		6.5	4.0		12.0			
H XIIIb	7.2	2.3	7.2	37.8	70		20.0	1.4		7.0			
H XIV	16.0			15.76	18		5.0	16.2		18.0			
H XVIIIa	40.0			150.0	24.3		8.0	10.7		16.0			
H XVIIIb	30.0												

*Calculated.
1/4 CHORD SWEEP BACK is 28 degrees from rib 7 to rib 17. Inboard it reduces to zero at the centre line, and outboard curves relative to tip shape.
DIHEDRAL is 4 degrees on the 'Wing Construction Datum Plane' which corresponds to the main lower boom.
The effective dihedral on the aerofoil datums varies from 3.5 degrees between rib 7 and the tip, to zero between rib 3 and the centre rib.

Weight empty - Kg	Weight of fuel - Kg	Take-off weight - Kg	Wing loading - Kg/m²	Power to weight ratio Kg/hp (Thrust to weight ratio, Kg/Kg) at take-off	Landing speed - Km/h	Maximum speed - Km/h	Minimum sinking speed, m/s, at speed - Km/h	Best gliding ratio	Power units
120	-	210	10.0	-	60	170	0.80/60	21	-
220	-	300	9.4	-	40	230	0.70/60	24	-
275	20	375	11.7	4.7	49	200	0.85/60	24	Hirth HM60R, 79 hp
250	-	330	10.3	-	42	230	0.70/60	24	-
220	-	300	8.3	-	37	210	0.48/45	28	-
250	-	330	8.8	-	39	210	0.50/45	28	-
300	40	420	11.2	9.5/6.6	44	160	0.60/53	25	Walter Mikron, Zundapp, 44/64 hp
340	30	450	11.1	15.2	46	140	0.60/53	28	Volkswagen KdF, 29.5 hp
280	-	360	9.6	-	41	210	0.52/47	28	-
300	-	460	12.2	-	46	210	0.60/53	28	-
250	-	330	17.5	-	55	200	0.50/60	37	-
270	-	350	18.5	-	60	200	0.45/70		-
1600	80	1840	54.0	11.6	84	280	-		2 x Hirth HM60R, 79 hp
1360	80	1600	42.0	10.1	70	260		-	2 x Hirth HM60R, 79 hp
1440	80	1600	42.0	10.1	70	260			2 x Hirth HM60R, 79 hp
330	-	410	23.0		64	200	0.45/70	45	-
1550	290	2000	45.5	4.2	77	350		-	2 x Argus As 10, 236 hp
5000	2760	8200	55.0	5.8	80	280*		-	6 x Argus As 10, 236 hp
1900	-	2000	43.5	-	75				-
4844	1700	6876	130.0	0.26	130	795	-		2 x Jumo 109-004B, 890 kg
	2000	7515	142.0	0.24	157	840*		-	2 x Jumo 109-004B, 890 kg
									BMW 109-003, 800 kg
460	80	700	32.3	7.9	75	200*	-		DKW, 88.5 hp
250	-	330	9.2		44	180	1.1/60	16	-
600	-	700	18.5	-	88	1100*	2.0/70	9	-
150	-	230	14.6		41	250*	0.55/55	30	-
11000	16000	32000	213	0.17	136	820*			6 x Jumo 109-004B, 890 kg
		33100		0.16		860*			4 x HeS 109-011A, 1300 kg

Endnotes

Introduction

[1] Patent Nr.253788. *Gleitflieger mit zur Aufnahme von nicht Auftrieb erzeugenden Hohlkorpen./*H. Junkers. 1.02.1910.

Chapter One - Fledged in the Third Reich

[2] *Schwanzlose Flugzeuge von Karl Nickel und Michael Wohlfahrt.*

[3] *Nurflügel.* Reimar Horten, Peter F. Selinger. Herbert Weishaupt Verlag. Graz, 1983.

[4] Memorandum. *Die Horten Nurflügel Flugzeuge. Erinnerungen von Karl Nickel.* (unpublished), September 2005.

[5] Hans Multhopp, *Die Berechnung der Auftriebsverteilung von Tragflügeln,* Luftfahrt Forschung 15 (1938), 153-169.

[6] The waggle-tip control was later tried again in an H III glider without much success due to the considerable control inertia. A further version of the single-control system was also considered with free-floating spring-loaded waggle-tips combined with drag rudders.

[7] The same type number was later assigned to the Blohm & Voss Bv 250, which may indicate that Luftwaffe never officially adopted the H IIIb – or the 'Ho 250'. In the RLM nomenclature the '8' prefix was applied to every aircraft regardless of its manufacturer.

[8] The RLM designation 8-252 was reallocated to the Junkers Ju 252.

Chapter Two - Nurflügel goes to War

[9] *Bierzeitung Sonderkommando* Lln.3 07-09-1942.

[10] It was nicknamed *'Die Butterfliege'* because Heinz Scheidhauer used to fly the H IIId at the end of the days on which he conducted his test flights, in order to secure an extra portion of rationed butter that was allocated to pilots who flew more than four hours a day. After reaching the four hour mark, he promptly came down to collect his extra ration.

Chapter Three - A Bomber for England

[11] Probably during the 18 March 1943 conference at Karinhall hunting lodge.

[12] Milch archives, cited in *The Rise and Fall of the Luftwaffe: The Life of Field Marshal Erhard Milch,* David Irving, 1973.

[13] The first operational fighter-bomber to conform to the "1000-1000-1000" criteria was the Republic F-84F Thunderstreak of early 1950's.

[14] The following types of fuel could be used with the Jumo 109-004 engines: B4 aviation fuel (specific gravity 0.75 kg/dm3), J2 synthetic fuel (0.83 kg/dm3), diesel fuel K1 or crude oil I2. Since the latter was in short supply at the end of the war, it was mostly J2 that was available, being manufactured from coal. When using fuels other than aviation fuel, the latter (B4 or B5) was used as a start-up fuel; after reaching 6000 rpm the engines switched automatically to main fuel. The Riedel two-stroke starter motor was fuelled by B4 or J2 mixed with motor oil.

[15] Letter from Karl Nickel to Captain Eric Brown, 08-04-1999.

[16] Development of the Horten flying wing aircraft. Paper by Karl Nickel (unpublished), 16 March 2006.

[17] *Nurflügel.* Reimar Horten, Peter F. Selinger. Herbert Weishaupt Verlag. Graz, 1983.

[18] Available photographs show torque scissors of at least two different designs mounted to the nose wheel of the H IX V1 during the tests.

[19] DVL - Berlin Adlershof betr. *Kurzbericht über Flugeigenschaftsmessung an Muster Horten IX V I.*

[20] According to Karl Nickel, the Dutch roll was never encountered in any Horten aircraft. A markedly different impression on handling characteristics of the Horten aircraft was presented by Eric Brown, who flew the H IV in 1947: "...on the advice of Scheidhauer I used the drag rudders as little as possible as this set up a Dutch roll... Certainly the Ho.IV had only marginal directional stability, and the use of the drag rudders gave yaw and pitch together, which set up a lazy sort of Dutch roll motion. Lateral control was sluggish but produced no adverse yaw..." *(Wings of the Weird & Wonderful,* Airlife Publishing, Shrewsbury, England, 1983.). Possibly the contradiction in views comes from different piloting practices, as noted by Karl Nickel in his unpublished *Memorandum, Die Horten Nurflügel Flugzeuge. Erinnerungen.* September 2005.

[21] Probably one of the early prototypes powered by the A-series Jumo 109-004.

Chapter Four - A Batwing from Gotha City

[22] Internal SS correspondence of 6 June 1944 states that the SS should "protect" the concept of Nurflügel aircraft.

[23] In various wartime documents the aircraft was alternatively designated as '8-229', Ho 229, Go 229 or Go 8-229.

[24] *Besprechungsniederschrift betr. Ho 229.* GWF, 7. Sept. 1944; *Fachgruppenarbeit für Attrappe in Gotha/*Rechlin E-2. 10. Sept. 1944.

[25] *Protokoll betr. Führerhaube, Ausrüstung,* etc. 23. Nov. 1944.

[26] The same size wheels were used also for the main landing gears of the Do 335 and Fw 190D respectively.

[27] *Wochenbericht Rechlin E 2.* 18.-25 Nov. 1944.

[28] *Kurz-Baubeschreibung Gotha 229 V 6.* 15. Nov.1944.

[29] *Reisebericht zu Askania betr. Einbau EZ 42 in 8-229.* 14. Nov. 1944.

[30] *Protokoll betr. Kurssteuereinbau in Ho 229.* 19. Okt. 1944.

[31] Autobiography by Erich Sommer (unpublished), via Alan Scheckenbach; *Reisebericht betr. Besuch bei Fa. Horten in Göttingen,* 28 Juni 1944.

[32] By this time the experience with the Me 328 and the manned version of the Fieseler Fi 103 flying-bomb showed that the pulse-jet was unsuitable for manned aircraft because of the excessive vibrations it developed.

[33] The original 8-254 number was reallocated to a Kurt Tank design; number 8-226 had been previously allocated to a Blohm und Voß project that later became the BV 246. At some point in 1944 this designation was applied also to the Focke Wulf project Fw 226 'Flitzer', later abandoned.

[34] *'Desarrollo de aviones rapidos sin cola',* by Dr. Reimar Horten, *Revista Nacional de Aeronautica,* September 1952, Buenos Aires, Argentina.

[35] Reimar and Walter Horten Interviews by David Myhra, transcription by Russel Lee, NASM Archives, Accession No. 1999-0065

[36] *Wochenbericht Rechlin E 2 betr. erster Standlauf Triebwerke in 229 V 2.* 23. Dez. 1944.

[37] A similar modular layout had been proposed earlier in the Fieseler Fi 333 project and actually tested in 1951 in the prototype Fairchild XC-120 Packplane.

Chapter Five - The Last Stronghold in Thuringia

[38] *Kriegstagebuch Chef TLR betr. notdürftig über-arbeitete Horten-Unterlagen.* 14. Jan.1945.

[39] *Gegenüberstellung 8-229/Go P-60.* Gothaer Waggonfabrik, A.G. Flugzeugbau-Entwicklung.

[40] Insufficient directional stability was one of the causes of failure of the Northrop B-35/B-49 programme.

[41] Ziller continued his training in single H IX V1 flights on 6 January, 2 and 8 February 1945 and performed several H VII flights in the end of January.

[42] RLM representative *Flugingenieur* Franz Binder was present during the H IX V2 tests.

[43] 1000 m to 1250 m according to other sources.

[44] Apart from the Province of Thuringia and the REIMAHG, Sauckel also controlled slave labour in Germany.

[45] *Projektvergleich der Jägervariante 8-229 und P 60*, DVL Berlin-Adlershof, 16 Feb. 1945.

[46] *Stellungnahme zum Project 'Gotha P.60'.* Horten, Göttingen, 16. Feb. 1945.

[47] *Einige Bemerkungen zur Stellungnahme von Horten zum Project 'Gotha P.60' vom 16.2.45.* Gothaer Waggonfabrik A.-G. Flugzeugbau – Entwicklung. 22. Feb. 1945.

[48] *Aktenvermerk über die Vorbesichtigung der Attrappe V 6. Wundes*, GWF, 22. Feb. 1945.

[49] H IXb drawing, 15 Feb. 1945; *Projektbaubeschreibung 2-sitzer Horten Zerstörer.* 1 March 1945.

[50] Similarly, the Me 262's hydraulic pump was fitted to one (port) engine only; the possible reason was wartime economizing. It was intended to later equip both engines with the pumps.

[51] *Versuchbericht Nr.925.229, 229 – Versuche mit Schleudersitz 8-229.16-Z01 (Funktionserprobung).* Feldinger, Feb.1945.

[52] Walter Horten suspected sabotage as a cause of the H IX V2 crash, e.g. someone placing a rag in the engine's oil tank that would inflict an acute oil failure and subsequent overheating. Although there was apparently no prove for this version, otherwise examples of sabotage were numerous within the late-war German aircraft industry, which used forced labour in large extent, even at critical production stages.

[53] Walter Horter in his later recollections suggested that the H IX V1 was air-towed to Brandis by a He 111.

[54] *Einsatzbereitschaftsmeldungen der Verbände der Lfl. Reich für die erste Hälfte April 1945 betr. Umschulung JG 400 auf Ho 229.*

[55] Reimar and Walter Horten interviews by David Myhra, transcription by Russel Lee, NASM Archives, Accession No. 1999-0065.

[56] *Eintrag im Kriegstagebuch Chef/TLR betr. fehlerhafter Unter-lagen der Gebr. Horten.* 25. Feb. 1945.

[57] Some sources quote the conference as being held on 20-23 February 1945 in Dessau.

[58] *Besprechungsnotiz betr. Besprechung Gebr. Horten /RM Göring.* 12. Mär. 1945

[59] There were also other range estimates, some as optimistic as 11,000 km. It should be remembered however that the H XVIII's real-life contemporary Northrop YB-49 all-wing bomber had twice the take-off weight and power to attain a comparable range – which was still insufficient for a return transatlantic flight.

[60] *Veleritos 'Sin Cola'* by Reimar Horten, *Revista Nacional de Aeronautica,* October 1949, Buenos Aires, Argentina.

Chapter Six - Reaching Enemy Soil

[61] CIOS report by F/Lt. D.C. Appleyard, Lt.Cmdr. M.A. Biot, May 1945;
Bolling AFH, Reel A5720, Frame 1897, Items for Weekly Activity Report, T.LD., 23 March 1945.

[62] Private communication from Gunilde Nickel, born Horten.

[63] Maxwell AFHO, 45th Depot Repair Station, April 1945, Historical Report, History of the Air Disarmament Division, 9th Air AFSC.

[64] Probably the mock-up of the 8-229V6 or Go P-53 or possibly Go P-60.

[65] McDonald, Technical Intelligence Report No. A-383, 10 May 1945, Subject: Inspection of Enemy Airfield.

[66] Sheldon, Technical Intelligence Report No. I-4, Hotrod [sic] 229 Bat Wing Construction, 12 May 1945. Basic report prepared by Herbert R. Haze.
"Technical Intelligence Report I-3, 19 May 1945, Subject: Interrogation of Herr Eckhardt Kaufmann Concerning Ho 229 Aircraft," 1-2, source unknown.

[67] RG 255, Box 231, Technical Intelligence Report No. I-I 1.
Interviews with Horten Brothers, Dr. Lambricht, and Dr. Madelung in London on
21 May 1945; Eric Brown, *Wings on My Sleeve*, Airlife: Shrewsbury, England, 1961, 82-83.)

[68] Bolling AFH, Reel 5720, Frame 0057, Daily Activity Report - Technical Intelligence-28 May 1945.
Bolling AFH, Reel 5720, Frame 0025, Daily Activity Report-Technical Intelligence-30 May 1945.
Bolling AFH, Reel 5720, Frame 0120.
Bolling AFH, Reel 5720, Frame 0801, Daily Activity Report-Technical Intelligence-2 June 1945.

[69] Bolling AFH, Reel 5720, Frame 819, Daily Activity Report-Technical Intelligence-1 June 1945.

[70] From article by Charles Prower in Aeroplane Monthly - September 1993 issue.

[71] The Horten Tailless Aircraft. K.G.Wilkinson. Royal Aircraft Establishment, October 1945.; 8. Bolling AFH, Reel 5720, Frame 0659, Daily Activity Report-Technical Intelligence-11 June 1945. Note that the WNr.31 was repeatedly referred to as H IIIg in the reports.

[72] McDonald, "Technical Intelligence Report No. A-461, Horten VI Tailless Sailplane," 22 June 1945. Basic report prepared by 1st Lt. William Parnicky.

[73] HQ Berlin Command, Office of Military Government for Germany (US) to Deputy Director of Intelligence European Command, Frankfurt, 16 December 1947.

[74] Bolling AFH, Reel 5720, Frame 0605, Daily Activity Report-Technical Intelligence-14 June 1945.
Bolling AFH, Reel 5720, Frame 0580, Daily Activity Report-Technical Intelligence-15 June 1945.

[75] Bolling AFH, Reel A5720, F0383, Daily Activity Report-Technical Intelligence-23 June 1945.

Boliing AFH, Reel A5720, F0358, Daily Activity Report-Technical Intelligence-26 June 1945.

Bolling AFH, Reel A5720, F0296, Daily Activity Report-Technical Intelligence-29 June 1945.

Bolling AFH, RA5720, Frame 1763, Weekly Activity Report-Technical Inteliigence-26 June 1945.

[76] Bolling AFH, Reel A5700, Frame 1280, General Summary of Technical Exploitation - Aircraft Design and General Aerodynamics.

[77] Inventory of G.A.F. equipment from 45th A.D.G. APO - U.S. Army. Shipped on 26 June to Port Transportation Officer, Cherbourg, France.

[78] Bolling AFH, Reel A5720, Frame 1575, McDonald to Statistical Control Office, HQ, USSAFE, Off. of Asst. Chief of Staff A-2, 13 July 1945, Weekly Activity Report for period ending 2400 hours, 12 July 1945.

[79] Letter from Captain Eric Brown. 29 November 1998.

[80] Extracts from a letter from Eric Brown to Paul Williams. 8 May 1978; 20 July 1982.

[81] Robert Kronfeld was an Austrian glider expert and chief test pilot of General Aircraft Ltd. He was killed in an air accident on 12 February 1948 while testing the experimental GAL-56 tailles glider.

[82] Extracts from a letter from Eric Brown to Paul Williams. 8 May 1978; 20 July 1982.

[83] David H. Baker, History of the Air Disarmament Division, 19 AFHO, Bolling, Reel C5034, Frame 1229.

[84] Dorney to Ross memorandum, 28 January 1946, "386.3 – Captured Enemy Equipment – Freeman Field 1945-46," RD 3737 (Box 3485), Sarah Clark Collection, RG 342, National Archives and Records Administration, Suitland, Maryland.

[85] *War Prizes* by Phil Butler, Midland Counties Publications, 1994.

[86] Memorandum. *Die Horten Nurflügel Flugzeuge. Erinnerungen von Karl Nickel.* (unpublished), September 2005.

Epilogue - Invisible Legacy

[87] Reimar and Walter Horten Interviews by David Myhra, transcription by Russel Lee, NASM Archives, Accession No. 1999-0065.

[88] GL conf, 24 Apr 1942. Milch archives, cited from *The Rise and Fall of the Luftwaffe: The Life of Field Marshal Erhard Milch.* David Irving, Focal Point, 1973.

[89] Ala volante Caza 'Horten IX'. Reimar Horten, *Revista Nacional de Aeronautica*, May 1950, Buenos Aires, Argentina.

[90] Nurflügel. Reimar Horten, Peter F. Selinger. Herbert Weishaupt Verlag. Graz, 1983.

[91] Reimar and Walter Horten Interviews by David Myhra, transcription by Russel Lee, NASM Archives, Accession No. 1999-0065.

Nurflügel: Die Geschichte der Horten-Flugzeuge 1933-1960. Reimar Horten, Peter F. Selinger. Herbert Weishaupt Verlag. Graz, 1983.

Reimar and Walter Horten interviews by David Myhra, transcription by Russell E. Lee, NASM Archives, Accession No. 1999-0065.

Veleritos 'Sin Cola'. Reimar Horten, *Revista Nacional de Aeronautica*, October 1949, Buenos Aires, Argentina.

Ala volante Caza 'Horten IX'. Reimar Horten, *Revista Nacional de Aeronautica,* May 1950, Buenos Aires, Argentina.

Planeadores 'Alas Volantes'. Reimar Horten, *Revista Nacional de Aeronautica,* October 1953, Buenos Aires, Argentina.

Desarrollo de aviones rapidos sin cola. Reimar Horten, *Revista Nacional de Aeronautica*, September 1952, Buenos Aires, Argentina.

Lift Distribution on Flying Wing Aircraft. Reimar Horten, *Soaring*, June 1981.

The World of Wings. R.G. Naugle, Flying, August 1949.

Wings of the Weird & Wonderful. Eric Brown. Airlife. Shrewsbury, England, 1983.

Wings on My Sleeve. Eric Brown. Airlife. Shrewsbury, England, 1961.

Warplanes of the Third Reich. William Green. Doubleday, N.Y., 1970.

Der Hornberg. Gerd Zipper, Aviatic Verlag, 1992.

The Horten Flying Wing in World War II. H. P. Dabrowski. Shiffer Military History v.47.

Jet Planes of the Third Reich, The Secret Projects, Vol. 1. Manfred Griehl, T. H. Hitchcock Monogram Aviation Publications, 1999.

German Aircraft Interiors, 1935-1945, Vol. 1. Kenneth A. Merrick, Thomas H. Hitchcock (Editor). Monogram Aviation Publications, 1996.

Horten Exotica...to the H IX and beyond. William Green, Gordon Swanborough. Air Enthusiast #39, May-August 1989.

Horten Aircraft. H. P. Dabrowski. Flug Revue 8-9/99.

Luftfahrt History Volume 9 *(Gotha Go (Ho) 229 + Horten Ho XIII)*, 2006.

Horten 229. Monogram Close-Up 12. David Myhra. Monogram Aviation Publications, 1983.

The Horten Brothers and Their All-Wing Aircraft. David Myhra. Shiffer Publishing, 1999.

The Horten Ho 9 / Ho 229 Retrospective. David Myhra. Schiffer Publishing, 2002.

The Horten Ho 9 / Ho 229 Technical History. David Myhra. Schiffer Publishing, 2002.

Junkers Ju 287. Horst Lommel. Aviatic Verlag, 2003.

Bonn-Hangelar, Band 2, 1926-1936. Hartmut Küper. Rheinlandia Verlag, 2005.

Ein Dreieck Fliegt. Alexander Lippisch. Motorbuch Verlag, 1976.

Göttingen im Luftkrieg 1935-1945. Martin Heinzelmann. Verlag die Werkstatt, 2003.

War Prizes. Phil Butler. Midland Counties Publications, 1994.

Luftwaffe '45. Manfred Griehl. Motorbuch Verlag, 2005.

Gotha die Fliegerstadt. Heiko Stasjulevics Gotha Kultur, Museum für Regionalgeschichte und Volkskunde Gotha, 2001.

Schwanzlose Flugzeuge. Karl Nickel, Michael Wohlfahrt. Birkhaüser, 1990.

Erinnerungen. Alexander Lippisch. Luftfahrtverlag Axel Zuerl, undated,

The Rise and Fall of the Luftwaffe: The Life of Field Marshal Erhard Milch. David Irving, Focal Point, 1973.

Reimar and Walter Horten interviews by David Myhra: transcription by Russell E. Lee, NASM Archives, Accession No. 1999-0065.

Ten Years Development of the Flying Wing High-Speed Fighter, paper presented by Horten Brothers, Bonn, before the Flying Wing Seminar, 14 April 1943.

Flugbuch of Lt. Erwin Ziller.

Besprechungsniederschrift betr. Ho 229. GWF, 7 September 1944.

Besprechungsniederschrift betr. Katapultsitz. GWF, 8 September 1944.

Bericht Nr.42, RLM Entvicklungsbesprechung. 29 October 1943.

Vorläufige Baubeschreibung 8-229. 22. November 1944.

Kurz-Baubeschreibung Gotha 229 V 6. 15. November 1944.

Wochenbericht Rechlin E 2 betr. erster Standlauf Triebwerke in 229 V 2. 23. Dezember 1944.

Gegenuberstellüng 8-229/Go P-60. GWF Flugzeugbau-Entwicklung, 27 January 1945.

Autobiography by Erich Sommer (unpublished), via Alan Scheckenbach.

Projektvergleich der Jägervariante 8-229 und P.60, DVL Berlin-Adlershof, 16 February 1945.

Stellungnahme zum Project, Gotha P.60'. Horten, Göttingen, 16 February 1945.

Einige Bemerkungen zur Stellungnahme von Horten zum Project Gotha P.60" vom 16.2.45. Gothaer Waggonfabrik A.G. Flugzeugbau – Entwicklung. 22 February 1945.

Aktenvermerk über die Vorbesichtigung der Attrappe V 6. Wundes, GWF, 22 February 1945.

Versuchbericht Nr.925.229, 229 – Versuche mit Schleudersitz 8-229.16-Z01 (Funktionserprobung). Feldinger, February 1945.

Kriegstagebuch Chef TLR betr. notdürftig über-arbeitete Horten-Unterlagen. 14 January 1945.

Triebwerkseinbau in Go 229 (Horten) (V3 u. V5). Junkers Flugzeug und motorenwerke A.G., 7 March 1945

The Delta Tailless Aircraft. A.D.I.(K) Report, 26 March 1945.

The Horten Tailless Aircraft. CIOS report by F/Lt. D.C. Appleyard, Lt.Cmdr. M.A. Biot, May 1945.

The Horten Tailless Aircraft. K.G. Wilkinson, Royal Aircraft Establishment Technical Note. Aero 1703 October 1945.

German Flying Wings Designed by Horten Brothers. ATI report by N. LeBlanc, 10 January 1946.

Memorandum. *Die Horten Nurflügel Flugzeuge. Erinnerungen von Karl Nickel.* (unpublished), September 2005.

Development of the Horten flying wing aircraft. Paper by Prof. Dr. Karl Nickel (unpublished), 16 March 2006.

Index